ABDUCTED IN
IRAQ

ABDUCTED IN
IRAQ

A PRIEST IN BAGHDAD

SAAD SIROP HANNA

with Edward S. Aris

FOREWORD BY DAVID ALTON

University of Notre Dame Press

Notre Dame, Indiana

University of Notre Dame Press
Notre Dame, Indiana 46556
undpress.nd.edu

Library of Congress Cataloging-in-Publication Data

Names: Hanna, Saad Sirop, author.
Title: Abducted in Iraq : a priest in Baghdad / Saad Sirop Hanna, with
Edward S. Aris ; foreword by David Alton.
Description: Notre Dame : University of Notre Dame Press, 2017. |
Identifiers: LCCN 2017024224 (print) | LCCN 2017034145 (ebook) | ISBN
9780268102951 (pdf) | ISBN 9780268102968 (epub) | ISBN 9780268102937
(hardcover : alk. paper)
Subjects: LCSH: Hanna, Saad Sirop. | Catholic
Church—Priests—Iraq—Biography. | Abduction—Iraq. | Iraq—Church
history. | Persecution. | Islamic fundamentalism. | Christianity and other
religions—Islam. | Islam—Relations—Christianity.
Classification: LCC BX1625 (ebook) | LCC BX1625 . H36 2017 (print) | DDC
282.092 [B] — dc23
LC record available at https://lccn.loc.gov/2017024224

∞*This paper meets the requirements of ANSI/NISO Z39.48-1992*
(Permanence of Paper).

to Dr. Sabah Aris

Contents

Foreword

David Alton

Born in Baghdad in 1972, Father Saad Sirop Hanna was ordained to the priesthood in 2001. Titular bishop of Hirta since 2014, he also serves as the auxiliary bishop of Babylon—a title that, along with remote Christian villages on Iraq's Plain of Nineveh, reminds us of the area's strong biblical associations. Christians have lived in this part of the world for close to two thousand years, and many speak the Aramaic language of Jesus.

Bishop Hanna holds a doctorate in philosophy, a degree in aeronautical engineering, speaks four languages, and has published learned articles. However, his scholarship and learning are not the reasons why *Abducted in Iraq: A Priest in Baghdad* will be among your prized possessions. This beautiful book is the captivating story of a faithful Iraqi priest who was abducted and tortured, and who resolutely refused to betray his beliefs or to hate his captors. This is Father Hanna's personal story—autobiographical, but interwoven with insights into what has happened to the ancient churches of this benighted region and how we in the West, having accelerated the assault on Iraq's Christian community, have done precious little since then to protect Iraqi Christians or to champion their cause. Bishop Hanna's instructive story is the account of one man, but it is also the living history of a suffering and persecuted people.

Bishop Hanna's sobering account should challenge us, his readers, who live in the relative comfort and safety of the West, to reevaluate our dismal record in relation to the beleaguered Christians of the Middle East. The statistics tell their own distressing story. In 2003, before the Iraq War, around one and a half million Christians lived in Iraq, about 6 percent of the population. Some recent estimates have put the number of remaining Christians as low as 200,000. With the failure to create a stable and pluralistic Iraq, Christians and other minorities have been either killed, forced to convert, or have fled. The Patriarch of the Chaldean Church, Louis Sako, has stated that this war of attrition means that for the first time in Iraq's history there are now no Christians left in Mosul—Iraq's second largest city.

In *Abducted in Iraq: A Priest in Baghdad*, Father Hanna narrates how his captors repeatedly told him—as they beat him with the butt of a gun—"you will be a Muslim," to which he replied, "la ikraha fid deen"—the verse from Islamic scripture which holds that no one can be forced or obliged to become a Muslim, that there is no compulsion in religion. Yet as his captors struck this blindfolded priest, they insisted on calling him a kafir, an infidel or unbeliever, warning him that if he failed to capitulate he would forfeit his life.

That these were not just rhetorical flourishes is illustrated in the beheading and mutilation of the Orthodox priest Boulos Iskander in the same year as Bishop Hanna's abduction. In 2008, Archbishop Paulos Faraj Rahho died after his capture in Mosul. In 2007, when Father Gassan Isam Bidawed Ganni was driving in Mosul with his three deacons, they were shot when they refused to convert to Islam. In 2010, an attack on an Assyrian Catholic church in Baghdad left fifty-eight people dead, including forty-one hostages and priests. Other Chaldean priests, deacons, and laypeople have suffered similar fates.

In flashback passages of his narrative, Bishop Hanna tells us that these escalating tragedies had their genesis with the events of September 11, 2001, which took the lives of 2,996 people and injured over 6,000 others. On that dreadful day the young Saad Hanna was in Italy, a seminarian studying for the priesthood. As he watched the unfolding horror of the Twin Towers, he remarked to his fellow seminarians, "the world is turning upside down. The Americans will not let this be."

The reader is left in no doubt that Bishop Hanna loves his country and believes that the absence of Christians will be bad for the Muslim population as well as a tragedy for the dispossessed. For the future, Bishop Hanna is clear that Christians in Iraq should favor a united Iraq and concentrate on promoting the idea of a citizenship that is not based on an ethnic or religious tradition; that Christians must adopt a language promoting unity; that they must work for a true and lasting reconciliation; that Christians in Iraq must be united and work together with all of the country's political parties, excluding no one person or group for ethnic or sectarian reasons; and that they must build a Christian politics that is faithful to the Gospel principles and the church's teachings.

Father Hanna further argues that Iraq's Christians have always lived in peace within the greater community and, over many centuries, have actively participated in the building of the nation—and must do so again. That he is ready to actively participate in this vision of reconciliation was clear from the moment of his ordination when he chose to return to Iraq. As he told the charity Aid to the Church in Need, "I love Iraq and I love my people, so I wanted to continue working here as a priest." He also believes that he has an appointed task to ensure that the West has a deeper understanding of the history of Christians in Iraq: "They do not know who we are, how we live here, what we do here. . . . It is so important to exchange ideas in order to understand how faith has been implemented in different societies." It was his very love for and commitment to his people and his country that probably saved his own life. The conversations Father Hanna had with one of his guards, Abu Hamid, and that guard's small acts of kindness are a timely reminder that, even in the heart of darkness, the small light of human compassion can burn.

Bishop Hanna's testimony and story deserve to be read by anyone who has ever wondered how they would react if they were kidnapped, tortured, told to abjure their faith, and faced likely death. It should be read by anyone with even a passing interest in the violence and hatred that have disfigured Iraq and now disfigure Syria. It should be read by anyone interested in the widely dishonored Article 18 of the Universal Declaration of Human Rights—born in the ashes of Auschwitz—which asserts our right to freedom of religion or belief. And it should be read by anyone who feels they need to be better informed about the ancient churches of the Middle East and the existential threat which these Christians face.

David Alton has served as Professor of Citizenship at Liverpool John Moores University and is a board member of the charity Aid to the Church in Need. Co-founder of Jubilee Campaign, he has been a member of the British Parliament since 1979 and an Independent member of the House of Lords since 1997.

Prologue

"The Lord is my shepherd, I shall not want. . . ."

Time is not a constant tick. Some minutes fall to the ground unnoticed, while others like windswept leaves turn and linger. The car was speeding on, and the world was spinning away beside it.

"He maketh me to lie down in green pastures, he leadeth me beside the still waters. He restoreth my soul. He leadeth me in the paths of righteousness for his name's sake. . . ."

My eyes closed and opened, pressed so close to my folded arms in the confines of my space that I saw only the blurry dirt of the backseat carpet.

"Yea, though I walk through the valley of the shadow of death, I will fear no evil: for thou art with me; thy rod and thy staff comfort me. . . ."

My stomach lurched as the car turned sharply and hurtled forward. Forward and away. Forward to a place I dared not yet think of.

"Thou preparest a table before me in the presence of mine enemies: thou anointest my head with oil; my cup runneth over."

I could not tell if I were speaking the words aloud, or if they were merely rattling inside me. I could not tell until the butt of the gun crashed down on my head and stirred the sense of the nightmare fast unfolding.

"Quiet!" the man above me barked, his voice ringing out through the deafening noise of the spinning wheels, the roaring engine, and the gravelly road beneath them.

"Quiet or by God right here I'll scatter your head!" he ordered, pressing the weight of his gun on the base of my skull in warning.

"The Lord is my shepherd. . . ." My voice fell. I closed my eyes once more and yet my lips continued moving. For fifteen minutes, I read and reread the psalm of David from my memory. In the whisper of a murmur, I wrapped myself in the lines and held onto the words like a man clinging to a torch as he plummets through the darkness.

Time is not a constant tick. I thought it had been traveling fast back then, too fast to hold on to and to decipher, but how could it have been? When to this day I close my eyes and still see every moment.

CHAPTER I

The Sign and the Soccer Field

August 12, 2006. I awoke at the bang outside. In all likelihood, it was not the first that night, only the latest in a series. Each a hand knocking at the door of my dreams until my eyes opened to let it enter.

Standing a little to the side, I peered out cautiously from the window, searching for the source of the commotion. A day would come when stray bullets would break the glass and all but destroy the room in which I was then standing, piercing through the pages of the books I kept on the shelves beside me. A holy book ripped by the bullets of men firing through the darkness. I remember staring at the bent and broken pages and seeing a kind of artistry in them. An artistic statement, perhaps too obvious for the galleries of the European cities I had visited, and yet not one made within the space of a studio, not made with precision but through the absence of it. That was much of Iraq in those days, change without precision. A knocking down of the walls that both held back and birthed the flood that then came raging.

There would be no bullets in my room that night. I listened for the next crack of gunfire, knowing I would not have long to wait, and when I heard it I, was reassured enough to return to my bed, to close my eyes and drift back to sleep.

There were two checkpoints near the Dora seminary that was my home, one closer than the other, and the attacks on them were nothing if not regular. A secular war was burning through the country, and the district of Dora, situated in southern Baghdad, had been described by the American soldiers serving at this time as "the most dangerous place in Iraq." The police officers occupying the checkpoints were not Americans but Iraqis. Shiite Muslims, who for long had been on the wrong side of power, were now forced to thwart the continuous attacks of the Sunni Muslims they had come to replace.

Three years earlier, in 2003, was the first time I heard gunfire in the night. I was not so casual about it then, but much of life is learning through experience, and some of the skills a man acquires are stranger than others. I would move to a place beside a window and listen to the pop and whizz of bullets. I would listen and ascertain which checkpoint was being hit and estimate the distance of the danger. Often I would call the young men who were our guards through the Walkie Talkies I had brought them, and they would tell me what they thought was happening. When the fighting was close, I would go to a room with no windows. There I would sit and again listen, hoping that the noise would not grow louder, waiting like someone cooking popcorn in the microwave, listening for the beats to become farther apart, to grow sparse and fade into silence.

That night, and the one that followed, the seminary was unusually empty. Father Zaid, the vice rector, had departed for his holidays, and Father Basil would not be arriving until the fourteenth. Solitude is a part of life for a priest, and yet it never ceases to offer its own hardships. When looking back at those two days spent alone in the midst of the turbulence of that time, I remember a nagging sense of uneasiness that rose up quietly within me, like the faint scratching of a forgotten thought, very close but out of reach. I look back upon those two simple days, and they seem a fitting prelude for what soon was coming.

When I was just a boy, there was a kind of book I liked. On each of its pages were fragments of a picture —a hand, a cloud, a feather, the door of a house—and all around these pieces was a jumble of numbered dots, some bunched together and some scattered, with no discernible pattern or reason for their order. But once you drew a line from dot one to dot two, from dot two to dot three, and so on, slowly, bit by bit, each stroke played its part to form a picture.

I had thought of it, at certain times more than others, had even had the question asked of me on occasion, and I suppose there would be a comfort in it, a lifting of the burden. Some might think that the religious are more likely to believe in fate. I, however, have never given myself over to the idea that life is preordained. Our lives are made up of choices intertwined with purpose. That freedom of choice is a trust and a burden passed from God to humankind, to place no fence along the path, to let us choose, and often choose wrong, to place no bounds on good or evil. Still, if there was ever an argument for fate, it would surely be made in hindsight, after the seemingly random dots have played their parts to form a picture. The truth is, I still think of it, and when I do, I think of two days in particular. I think of the sign in the store, and I remember a hot and seemingly ordinary afternoon, when God found me on a soccer field.

It is often through the inevitability of aging, of the way the world is, of what it may demand of us, and what we in turn grow to demand of ourselves, that the word *simple* becomes attached to the period of our youth. And yet simple is what that time was for me. I was raised in a simple home by a family of simple means, my days governed by simple youthful priorities.

Whenever I find myself transported back to the days of growing up in the home my father built, as I often do, and often did when my arms were bound and my eyes had no place to look but inward, I see a time that was as simple as it was beautiful.

Having six siblings, three older sisters, two older brothers, and one younger sister, I had a childhood filled with companionship.

Love, I am thankful to say, was not a concept I had to learn, but had always surrounded me.

We lived in an area called "Ghadeer" in the center of Baghdad. Tightly packed with flat-roofed houses, on the roofs of which the families often slept throughout the summer nights, it was neither a poor nor an affluent neighborhood. A place like much of the Baghdad of the time, where Christians and Muslims lived side by side without that fact ever earning them a sense of pride or achievement. It was just the local community.

My school was a twenty-minute walk from our house, and once class was over, I would race home to finish any work I had as quickly as possible, so I could join my friends, who at most times were already out. When people drove through our streets, they almost always did so at a creep, not only because the narrowness of the road barely allowed for two cars to pass one another, but because around every turn there might be a game of soccer in full swing.

The world moves quickly. There were no computers or phones for us to play with, and the endless choice of television channels we now enjoy was then far more limited. However, there were two shows that I would not miss that together tell a lot about the boy I was. The first, named *Science for All*, was a weekly report on the advancements the world was making. The wide array of subjects ranged from space voyages to complex surgery, and every Tuesday evening, I sat and watched in wonder, fascinated by the horizon of possibility. For as long as I can remember, I never found studies to be bothersome. Homework was not a chore that I did to appease my teachers or my parents, though they had instilled in me the necessity of education, and I did take much pride in showing them the results of my labors. More than that, though, I had a thirst for learning, for solving problems, for collecting the tools necessary for tackling whatever questions happened to be etched on the exam papers that were turned facedown, waiting to be turned in. Much of me has changed throughout the years, but the young boy eager to know more remains unaltered.

The second program, *Sport of the Week*, was shown on Friday evenings. It covered a wide array of sports, but my interests leaned toward one. Soccer. The Iraqi national team was a relatively strong force at the time. We had won the Arab Nations Cup twice, and I watched them lift it twice again in 1985 and 1988. In 1986, however, when I was fourteen years old, something quite remarkable happened. Even though the war with Iran was ongoing, forcing Iraq to play their home games at neutral venues, the team still managed to qualify for the World Cup in Mexico.

There is something different about these kinds of sporting occasions. Even as a boy I could feel it. It wasn't about who followed the sport and who didn't. That summer, everyone was a soccer fan. Iraq would go on to score the country's first, and to this day only, goal at a World Cup finals tournament, before falling in the group stage.

On the wall above the television set, where I would sit to watch my favorite shows on those Tuesday and Friday evenings, was a cross that my mother had proudly hung in our home. Our family was Chaldean Catholic, and religion was an important part of our everyday lives and our identity. My mother went to church on every Sunday and I, like my brothers and sisters before me, received my first Holy Communion at the age of eleven. Yet if you had asked that boy about the life he imagined his future would hold, his answer, among the many and varied possibilities, would certainly not have involved the priesthood.

Up to my late teens, my time continued to be divided, in the same way as my two favorite television shows, between soccer and learning. By that time I had grown to six feet in height, with a lean muscular physique, and had developed a reputation as both an able and a fierce competitor.

Those who know me now would be surprised to learn that it was not overly unusual for me to find myself in the middle of a fight, though I must say that most times it was because of my protective nature rather than malice. If I felt a friend of mine had been harshly tackled or kicked during a game, I was not shy about immediately intervening to even up the score. Meditation and calmness were yet to be my allies. More than that though, I was known to be one of the better soccer players in the neighborhood. For this reason, one afternoon, when I was seventeen, two boys who had been playing on the opposing team strolled over to speak to me after a game.

I knew their names, as I did most people in the local area. What they knew of me was that I was a good player and a Christian. As they jogged along beside me, one of them quickly asked if I had thought of playing for the church team. In truth I was out of breath, the Iraqi sun was scorching down, and I didn't feel much like breaking my step as I walked toward some shade, so I was barely listening. "What?" I asked.

"The church," the other boy repeated. "We have a very good team. We both play on it, why don't you come and play with us?"

Why not? I casually thought, and I was about to agree when I was struck with a reservation.

"I would," I said, "but do I then have to go to the church?"

"No!" the boy assured me, "you just have to come the once."

"Come on Friday," the other boy said. "Just register your name, one time and that's it, you'll be on the team."

I promised that I would and thought little of it. On the following Friday evening, after I had returned from school and finished whatever work I had, I made my way to the church to sign my name and join the team.

Though I knew it, to any others the church at the time was a difficult building to distinguish. There was no courtyard, no statues, no heavy stone walls, and no large cross on the rooftop. Instead it was a house, seemingly much like any other. This was for no real reason other than the scarcity of funding. In fact, on that Friday afternoon, at a different site from the one where I was headed, an actual church for the parish was midway through construction.

To my surprise, when I got there I found the place quite full of people close to my age. Young men and young women were busily taking their seats in the large room where mass was daily given, except there was no mass that day. Instead a catechism class was about to begin.

Curious, I wandered in and listened, and what I heard that day would change my life in the only way that lasting change can happen. The kind of change that we carry with us no matter where we go, the kind that may come from a lesson, an encounter, or an experience, but wherever it may come from, it brings with it more than a thought or a feeling, but a glimpse into a new way of seeing.

In Hebrew, the name Jesus means "God saves." I thought I had known much of my religion, but after no more than a few words and a few minutes, it seemed that I knew little. The priest spoke of the life of Christ, and how its message was less of commandments and far more of sacrifice and love. Jesus, the son of God made man to save his people.

When the class was over, I signed my name to the football team and left awash with an unfamiliar inspiration. Perhaps there are moments in our lives when we are searching for the answers without ever knowing we had asked the questions. It was not as people often imagine when thinking about how a man might first give himself to religion. It was not in the flash of an epiphany but in the slow and gradual possession of a purpose found. I submerged myself within it, dedicating time both to prayer and to learning, and the more I read of Christ, the more I grew to admire him. This quickly became my new routine. At home I would read and pray and then read some more. Stopping not at simply reading the words but delving deeper, always searching for the meaning, for the message and the teachings, for that all-encompassing reason, the truth.

Father Jameel Nissan was the priest at the time, and he allowed us to indulge in many initiatives. I began to attend prayer meetings, spiritual meetings, and prayer encounters. Soon enough I had developed many friendships, as my trips to the church continued to grow in frequency.

I watched Father Jameel, I watched the way he preached, taught, counseled, and helped his people, and I was moved by his example. For me it was not a case of simply becoming more religious or finding a greater belief in Christ. It was becoming increasingly apparent that the spiritual life was the life I wanted, and it was at this point that I began to feel a calling.

Three years from the day I went to the church to join their soccer team, I had decided to become a priest. What I had not done was tell anyone of my intention, and so one evening, while I was helping my father in his store, I felt the time had come to inform him of my decision and to seek his approval.

My father prized education. Though he worked long tiring hours in the local convenience store he owned and ran, he remained a voracious reader and instilled in me, and my brothers and sisters, the essential importance of knowledge.

After achieving high grades, I initially left Baghdad in 1990 to study medicine at the University of Dora. That change would however be a fleeting one as the Gulf War rendered the area too dangerous at the time, and I had to return to Baghdad after a mere two months. I was forced to change my degree to engineering in order to continue my studies there.

I can say with truth that, even if I had continued on the path of medicine, the priesthood would still have remained my final destination. In that respect, fate had no hand to play. It was only a small irony that I would leave Dora to escape from one danger, only to return a few years later to another.

On the day when I at last decided to tell my father of my decision to join the seminary, I was in my second year of university, studying aeronautical engineering. We had been working in the store for a few hours as I toyed with how to order my words, moving at times to speak, only to be interrupted by the entrance of a customer or by my own trepidation. The afternoon gave way to evening, and when a spell of prolonged silence had finally settled around us and we were both sitting behind the counter, having no shelves to stack or customers to serve, I simply came out and spoke two short sentences. "I want to leave college," I said. "I want to go to the seminary."

"Become a priest?" he asked for confirmation.

"Yes."

"No," he shook his head in short sharp movements, "no, no," his eyes circling the room for something to do as a way of signaling the end of the conversation. But it wasn't going to end there, and neither of us thought it would.

"This is not coming from now," I assured him. "From before I knew. I knew that this is what I want to do and now I want to do it."

"Become a priest!" he said again, dismissively.

"Yes."

"Look," he began, his voice at once less erratic, falling into that fatherly tone that merges thought-out advice and non-negotiable instruction seamlessly together, "finish your studies, get married, start a family and you can be the best priest for your own children."

"I have thought about it all, and that is not what I want to do!" I replied forcefully. "I don't want to finish these studies, I want to join the seminary. That is what I want to do."

"You have been studying for two years, and you want to stop now?"

Before I could answer, the door squeaked open and in walked Albert, a man who had grown up in the same village as my father. A long-time friend and a local priest.

Utterly undeterred by what might have been construed by some as a less-than-subtle sign, my father immediately turned to Father Albert for help in dissuading me.

"Come Father, come. My son," he said, pointing at me in exasperation, "he is telling me he wants to be a priest!"

Father Albert turned and looked at me, and with a faint smile and a slight nod, he said, "Why not?"

"Why not?" my Father repeated. "What why not? He is in the second year of his studies . . ."

His hands were gesturing in front of him, asking to be understood, and he paused to steady himself to continue the stream of reason. "He is young, let him get married, start a family, have some children, and then look after *them*."

It was not an unreasonable request. What father does not want his son to start a family? I knew it then, just as I know it now, the sacrifices of priesthood would not be mine alone.

"I am an only child," said Father Albert. "I have no brothers and no sisters. I am all my parents had, and they allowed me to become a priest. God gave you seven children. Three sons. Will you not give one to God?"

My father fell silent. He neither agreed nor made a gesture in that direction, but I could see that the argument of his friend had moved him.

Father Albert purchased what he had come to buy before leaving, and after a few minutes, of the two of us, it was my father who was the first to speak.

"We won't talk of this anymore," he said, "*but* you go on and finish your studies, and if you still want to, then we will talk again."

And that was that. We had made a deal, my father and I, one that we would both stick to. From the soccer field, to the priest in the store, I look back on the dots of my life and see myself sleeping in the seminary on that twelfth of August, three days before the Assumption feast and my abduction.

CHAPTER 2

On the day my life would be forever altered

On the fourteenth, a Monday, Father Basil returned to the seminary, and it was good to have some company again. That early evening we ate dinner together and went for a walk, where we spoke of many things and one in particular.

Throughout my travels, whenever I met someone new and told them a little about myself, the second of two facts would always be met with surprise. I say the second because which fact caused the surprise depended on the order. The first was always considered normal but not the second, because to the person asking, the second did not go with the first. I am a Christian; I am from Iraq. I am from Iraq; I am a Christian. This is quite understandable. When a country is far from the world in which you live, you often see it only through the context of the stories you come across. For those far away, the Christians of Iraq gained most prominence in the recent hours of their plight. I say hours only in comparison to the many years that mark their ancient history. The truth is Christians were in Iraq long before most other places, from the first century AD to the present day.

And in all that time, their numbers had never dwindled at a rate faster than in the years after the fall of Saddam Hussein in 2003.

We spoke of this unfolding issue, of its immense complexity, and of what could and could not be done. "Should we leave?" Our parishioners would ask. "It is not safe here for us anymore," they would protest.

What could we say to that?

On the first of August 2004, almost exactly two years and two weeks earlier, I had been conducting a mass in Dora, much as I did on any other Sunday. The time was six-thirty in the evening, and the service was an hour in when a sudden sound erupted with such power that the church stones shook inside its echoes. It is hard to describe such a sound. Neither loud nor deafening seem adequate, because the decibel level plays only a minor role in its measure. For far more than the noise itself is its meaning, and in the meaning are the rush of feelings wrenched to the fore in one cold moment. Fear, anger, and empathy are all suddenly alive and blind to their target.

That day. A Sunday. A series of explosives had been detonated across Iraq. All the targets were churches.

Six in all were simultaneously hit with car bombs in a coordinated attack that killed twelve people and injured seventy-one others. My church was not one of them, yet among those struck was the church of St. Paul and St. Peter, a mile or so away from where I was giving mass that same evening. I still remember standing beside the black shells of cars among the wreckage of the aftermath, and wondering what would become of our country.

I cannot say it is always so, but when a war is not waged on some unknown field beyond the borders of our land, when it lives and breathes among us, fear becomes the master of all things. It patrols the streets, it sits outside our doors, and it marks every corner. What is more, it walks beside every person we encounter. Suspicion grows, and divisions find new meanings. In times of travesty, blame is the most plentiful of resources.

Where are you from? Where were you raised? Are you a Christian or a Muslim? Sunni or Shiite? Arab or Kurdish?

Soon enough, men and women were slowly being stripped of their individuality, reduced to headlines of belief and birthright. In a time when our unity was most necessary for rebuilding for the future, where the monuments of the past and the ruins of the present could have fed the hope of a collective tomorrow, we were instead becoming foreigners to one another. In the land of fear, resentments can quickly bloom into hatred. We would look at one another and think, this person does not want me, this person does not like me. The Sunni Muslim, having been forced to relinquish power, would look at the Shiite, and see the person who had taken it. He would look too at the Christian, now cooperating with the Shiite government, and see him as his enemy. Likewise the Shiite Muslim would look at the Christian as someone who had once dealt with the Sunni and therefore cannot be trusted. And the Christian would look at both and feel that they detest him. So the biggest divide of all was growing in the hearts and minds of the people.

Life went on however, and despite the danger, the bombs, the attacks, and the growing spate of abductions, still people carried on with their lives as best they could, and still they hoped for a better future. I too hoped that the darkness would be a prelude to a new dawn breaking, and so I remained and can honestly say I was never tempted to leave, even when my mother and sisters, who had all moved abroad by then, insisted daily on the idea. I was needed here, and I went about the business of helping, assisting both the Christian families as well as an assortment of Muslim ones. Poverty and plight do not discriminate according to religion, and we endeavored to help where help was needed. Every month, in addition to assisting Christians, we would distribute aid in the form of money and food to between five and ten Muslim families in the neighborhood.

On that fourteenth of August, as Father Basil and I walked down the street beside the seminary, we spoke about the many errors that occurred after Saddam Hussein's departure. Of the dissolving of the army and the police without real alternatives, of the events of these days that fell like rocks on the back of our country. We spoke about the obstacles that cannot be easily negotiated, of the rotting of the meaning of our nation, of a people now divided by ethnicity and religion who are no longer simply Iraqi. We also spoke of the many Christians we lost from our community, if not through departures then most terribly through killings and kidnappings. We spoke of how unprepared the country and the church had been for what we then called democracy, and in particular we spoke of the role we could play for our people and how we could best promote unity. The Assumption feast was a part of that. It is a most significant day, as we Catholics believe that, having completed the course of her earthly life, the Virgin Mary was on the fifteenth of August assumed body and soul into heaven.

For much of the week prior, I had been busily making all the necessary arrangements for the occasion. I had met with my pastoral council, arranged the order and content of the mass, distributed readings among the deacons, and prepared a large table in the courtyard where we would all go at the end of the mass to enjoy the many dishes brought in by the members of our parish. That togetherness was the symbol of our unity, of the pastoral family and the spirit of giving.

Utterly unaware of what the next day would truly bring, after the walk with Father Basil I returned to my room and once more read over the words of my sermon, making whatever minor changes I felt were needed, before I went to sleep in anticipation of an early start the following morning.

I awoke at six o'clock on the day my life would be forever altered. I still recall the details, the minor pieces that I gathered up when all else seemed close to breaking. I showered and got dressed before having a breakfast of coffee, cheese, bread, and date syrup.

The church has a book that recommends suitable prayers for each day, and as I had no mass that morning, I began with a prayer from the book, before saying another of my own choosing. This was my regular routine, to read a passage of the Bible and then meditate on its meaning.

That morning, my choice was Luke 1, the Hymn of Mary.

Once my solitary prayers were over, I went to organize the preparations. Together, a number of volunteers from the parish and I cleaned the church, put the flowers on the altars, and arranged the tables in the yard for the food that would soon be coming. When the work was done and all was satisfactory, I took some time to sit with the guards, to drink tea and talk a little.

The state of the country in the aftermath of the war meant that there were few opportunities for work, and so when a decision was made, upon our request, that the churches be guarded by Christians and not Muslims, a sudden opening occurred for new employment. The agreement involved a month of mandatory training with the Iraqi police. On completion the candidates would become certified members of the Facilities Protection Service, earning a government wage of 200,000 Iraqi dinars per month, which is equivalent to approximately $US180. In addition, the church was given two Kalashnikov automatic rifles to be used by the service guards on duty. I placed a notice in the church to advertise the new positions, and waited for applicants. There were not many.

However, after some time we had gathered together six young men, from twenty to thirty years of age, and they became our guards. Alternating two-man shifts meant the church had an armed presence at all times. Using some of our funds, I built a small room for them, with a little fridge so they could store their food whenever they were on duty, and these same young men became my news portal to all the goings on in the neighborhood. Each day I sat with them a while and they would tell me not only of the incidents that had occurred but also of their lives and worries. Many had young families and were, like all of us, concerned about the fragility of the country's future. In truth their presence at our gate was mainly symbolic in nature, so that others would know that the place was not unattended. Though they were brave young men, their experience with firing a weapon was in most cases limited to the month's training they had taken.

I drank my tea and listened to them that day, quite unaware that I would soon be sat down beneath a tree, my eyes shrouded and my arms bound, listening to the young man who was my captor as he spoke of concerns not at all dissimilar to those voiced by the men charged with my protection.

At a few minutes before two in the afternoon, I drove my old white Toyota back to the seminary, where I had my lunch and took an hour's siesta. When I awoke at three thirty, I dressed and returned to church. The mass was to begin at five, but we opened the doors a half hour early so that people could come in and pray the rosary.

The church's capacity is 200. By five o'clock, as I entered and the mass began, there were 250 people in attendance. The pews were filled, and other people stood in rows along the walls to listen. In the midst of all the danger, still the people came, still they prayed, not only for what they wished for, but in thanks for what they had.

When the time came for me to speak, I aimed to give them hope. I spoke of the lives of Jesus Christ and the Virgin Mary, of how today as Christians we are called to walk the path of their example. How though the circumstances differ, the requirement is yet the same. How we are called to guard our faith, to believe and to uphold the principles and the meaning of what Christ our Lord had taught us, for to believe in him is to believe in love. That is the truth of his message. As he gave love and forgiveness to all, even those who aimed to do him harm, we too must endeavor to do likewise, no matter the obstacles.

I spoke of the hardship that the Virgin Mary was subjected to. A young girl pregnant with the Son of God. A Jew living in a land occupied by Romans. There was no security for her, as there is none for us either, and yet we place our faith in God as she did.

I was filled with joy that so many people had come to church that Tuesday evening, and I wished to give each of them back a piece of the strength their being there had given me. I ended by telling them that though we are fearful we are not afraid to give our lives for Christ.

Normally, I would stand beside the door to greet the people as they left. However, on this day, we all walked out together. The parishioners who had brought a dish had given it to one of our volunteers before the mass, and there was barely room enough on the tables we had set out that morning, so plentiful was the food that they had brought for one another.

The Iraqi sun never looks sideway and rarely whispers, but its heat had mellowed by that evening as we stood, ate, drank, spoke, and laughed together. It was not only the happiness of being together. It was more than that. I have borne witness to a variety of harsh circumstances in the world that were imposed upon people, most often through no fault or ill judgment on their part. When they live their lives beneath a shadow of unrelenting hardship, they find themselves stumbling onto moments filled with a pure and weightless joy that seems to transcend reason in its simplicity. But the reason is in an absence and a forgetting, and it is found by those who have learned to value what all of us at some point have taken for granted, normality.

At twenty minutes past seven, I returned inside, changed out of my robes, and then said my goodbyes and thanked those who had helped, and were still doing so, before I drove back to the seminary. As I left, two guards were beginning their shift for the night, and I told them to call me if anything were to happen. They waved and nodded at the familiar instruction, and I walked off to my white Toyota. I always parked it close, some twenty or so meters along the street on which the church was situated.

The keys were barely out of my pocket when I heard a voice behind me.

"Father, Father!" the young man called as he jogged down the road.

"Yes?" I asked.

"Father, are you going to the seminary?" I nodded. "Can I then get a ride with you, if that's alright?"

The young man, John, was a member of the parish, and I knew him, though not too well. His home was on the street behind the seminary. It was the first time he had ever asked me for a ride.

"Of course," I said, "come on in."

The street was empty, and I began the short drive home. I did not see them at first and then I did. John was saying something, but I had stopped listening, my eyes fixed on the rearview mirror, looking at the two cars rushing down the road toward us.

CHAPTER 3

I am here and this is real.
Be strong.

It was not the alertness that comes with fear but the one that comes with impending danger, and the two are not the same. I was not fearful then, and yet my senses narrowed, attending to little except what I could see fast approaching. Incidents of violence were far from uncommon, and as I had not yet seen any wreckage nor heard a sound, I presumed these cars were on their way to play some role in what would soon be coming. At no point did I even begin to think that they were coming for me.

With my eyes transfixed on the rearview mirror, I eased my foot off the gas, my hands gently turning the wheel to move the car from their path so they could continue unabated. The rest took place in distorted time, in the ebbs and flows that I would come to know with excruciating intimacy. First came the hypnotic seconds, descending down in slow rotations as the cars drew ever nearer and I sat watching and waiting for them to pass us by, to speed off without slowing. Waiting to watch the danger fade and disappear, but then came the screech, and the slow revolving seconds struck the ground to smash in all directions.

In a single moment, the two cars were beside me, and in the next, one of them had moved to the front and come to a sudden swerving stop. Barely had I lifted my foot from the brake when I heard the clicks of two doors opening from the car in front, and two more from the other close behind as four men leaped out and surrounded us.

Balaclavas, three shots, and Kalashnikovs. They were the first things I noticed. Three shots popping through the air in warning, and then the guns were back on us, always on us as the four men moved in apparent unison, only their wide white eyes and stern mouths visible through the hoods they wore.

This was no robbery.

"Get down!" one man shouted. "Get down from the car!"

"You are mistaken," I urged.

"Get down!"

I had let go of the wheel, and my hands were extended palm out in front of me. "Get down!" he ordered once again, the gun unwavering in his hand, its barrel staring back at me. I reached out and pushed the door open, and as I did so he briskly stepped forward and yanked me from the car.

"You," the other man said to John, "leave! We have nothing to do with you, go, go!" I looked up and saw him for only two brief moments. The first was when he hesitated, glancing back at me before he ran.

What else was he to do?

He was gone, and even then, even in the chaos of it all, while they pressed and pulled me by my neck to push me down into the car, as I cast my eye in that second moment to see him running down the street, I felt a strange flutter of relief bubble up from the sea of dread fast rising.

The Lord is my shepherd, I shall not want. . . .

As I lay on the backseat carpet, beside the boots of the men who had taken me, as I felt the weight of their rifles resting on my thigh and shoulder, those words came to me unbidden. Even as one of my captors struck me on the base of my skull, as he screamed his threats and the car sped off to some unknown place

I am here and this is real. Be strong.

and some unknown terror, still I held onto those words and still those words held onto me. Whenever the verse reached its end, I simply started over, and we continued in this way, the men saying little to each other, except the odd instruction of "faster" or "go," and me humming a quiet prayer, for roughly fifteen minutes, until the car slowed and came to a stop.

There is an odd awkwardness to keeping pace when being led by others. As I was pushed from the car, I could see we were parked on a trail surrounded by farmland, by tall grass, and by straw, with no homes or buildings. We had not yet reached our destination.

"You have made a mistake. . . ." I began once more in protest.

"Be quiet," the one hooded man replied. "Lower your head," ordered the other. And then suddenly it dawned on me, the very obvious truth of their not caring, not listening, and so I did as I was told. Perhaps a time would come for reason and argument, I thought. Until then I must comply in order to reach it. As one man pulled my arms behind my back, and I felt the pinch of handcuffs, another tied a thick black cloth across my eyes, and I was hustled into the boot of the car. Tucking my legs beneath my body so I would fit before the hood slammed shut to dim the darkness to blackness, and I felt the car speed off. The whole transition must have taken barely two minutes.

This second part of that awful drive was far longer, both by the true count of seconds, and more importantly by the feel of them. Adrenalin, fear, and confusion had flooded over me, each jostling for room in the cramped space I occupied. It was nearly forty degrees that night, and when melded with the heat from my own curled body and that generated by the running car, it had climbed far beyond the realm of the bearable. I lay slowly drowning in this metal box while the sound of the tires rubbing along on the dirt trail buzzed around me. As my body shook and bobbed, and the car sped on across the ditch-filled roads, I took shallow breaths and yearned for a gulp of air to steady me.

It was all going too fast, and I had yet to truly appreciate what was happening. *Be strong*, I repeated quietly to myself, thinking of what might soon be coming, of the questions I would ask if given the chance, and the answers I would give when I was undoubtedly questioned. *Be strong,* I said, and the thought helped nudge me from the airless present.

When you are waiting for the moment of a change, there is always a sudden second. A half hour or more had limped on by when I felt the car begin to slow. We were close. The ground crunched beneath the tires as we crept on to our destination. Until finally, we stopped.

My nerves began to stretch as I longed for the opening of the car boot, and likewise dreaded it. Footsteps sounded from differing directions, and the car doors thumped shut behind the men who had delivered me. With a creek, the lid of the metal box was opened to give me air but keep me in the darkness of the veil I wore. I felt the grip of fingers on my back and arms as I was lifted out and forward, my legs reaching down to find the ground and quickly succumbing as the two men pushed me to my knees. I knelt on that gravelly ground, my lungs pulling at the air in thirst and trepidation. No longer was it only the men who had captured me. I could not see but I heard and felt the presence of many others curiously surrounding me. It would be the first time I felt the palpable sensation of being watched without knowing from where, or having the option to turn in that direction.

"You are mistaken in taking me," I said to all and no one in particular.

"No," a man beside me tutted, "you will see, you wait and see. Soon you will be one of us, you will be a Muslim."

"I will not be a Muslim," I quickly answered.

The blow here came harder than the one I had received in the car. Blinded I could not see it coming. All I heard was a shuffle in the dirt before the butt of the gun struck me in the temple. With no arm to steady my fall, I crashed down sideways, wincing.

"You will see!" he hissed, his words dripping down with menace as he leaned in close over me. "Tomorrow, we will load you up for Hussainia. . . ."

"You be quiet!" a voice rang out from the distance. "Who are you? This is not your business. Leave him."

The man above me stopped, and I felt him draw away. "Bring him," came the order, and so I was brought, led forward step by step, with my hands behind my back, my head bowed, my eyes covered. I was ushered inside the home we had driven to. Moved through one room and then another, to the place where I would remain. Lowered onto a mattress on the floor before the door closed and all fell silent.

I half expected someone to walk in and ask me questions, for them to realize I was not the man they wanted, for this horrible mistake to be cleared up, with no apologies and no hard feelings. At the very least to offer an explanation. I very much felt the want of an explanation. But no one came.

With a twist, I sat up on the mattress, crossed my legs beneath me, and took a minute to simply breathe. It had all been so loud, the barking orders, the rustling of each move, and the incessant drive. One thing piling on the other, and the noise coming not only from what was audible but also from confusion, from fear, from the many parts of a drastic change in fortune. The feeling that you are being carried atop a wave unbreaking, as it carries you so very far from shore.

Though, because of the blindfold and the unlit room, I could not see, still I closed my eyes to better think, making the choice to alleviate the panic of what had been forced upon me. Slowly, I began to gather up all the words and events, to sift them through the sieve of thought and see what facts remained.

"Soon, you will be one of us," the man had said. "You will be a Muslim." *This was no mistake.* Perhaps they thought me more important than I was, but still they knew me, they knew that I was Christian, and no doubt they knew me to be a priest. "Tomorrow, we will load you up for Hussainia," he had gone on to say, this man who in his hatred toward me was answering my questions.

"Hussainia," is a collective name given to Shia mosques, derived from Husayn Ibn Ali, the grandson of the prophet

Mohammed, and the third imam of the Shia Muslims. What he was telling me was they would plant explosives on my person and effectively detonate me. I knew then that they were Sunni, and that fact worried me. That may seem strange, to find cause for increased alarm in the identity of my abductors, when the very fact that they had chosen to abduct me ought to have been ample reason for fear, for knowing them to be "bad" men who wished to do me harm. Yet there it was. To begin with, through the teachings of Christ, I do not see people as "good" and "bad," but I see the badness and the goodness of their actions. Knowing these men to be Sunni, I could make a guess at their probable motivations. There is a great difference between a gang and an ideological group, as the latter lends itself to the likelihood of fanaticism. These Sunni men may well have been Al Qaeda, followers of a branch of Sunni Islam known as Wahhabiyya. Named after Muhammad ibn Abd al-Wahhab, it is, simply put, a movement that aims to return Islam back to its original principles. Though there are debates on what the movement advocates with respect to the treatment of non-Muslims, my sitting bound and blindfolded did not bode well for the case of peaceful coexistence.

I thought of what this meant for me, and would take hold of my mind whenever it wandered into specifics, when it made the bloody footprints in the gore-filled details. There was an urge to imagine that too, to prepare for all eventualities, but even at this early stage, doing so seemed like a surrender. I endeavored to overcome, to move past this situation, and so I did what I have always done and turned to God for answers.

True prayer is not in the incanting of words. Ironically, in paying too much heed to the words of prayers, we pay them both more and less than their rightful share. To think that the words are the reason, that the words are the call, the point of contact, the way to the ear of God, and to the echo of his voice, reduces prayer to incantation, a series of words uttered repetitively to stir the spirit to waking. To pray is to listen. "What is your purpose in this?" I asked of God. "What do you want from me? What am I to do?" Again and again that night I asked, and felt inside the core of my faith that in time a light would shine upon the answers. *Tomorrow*, perhaps tomorrow.

I had never been one to bemoan the length of days. Long is good when there is much to do, just as tiredness is also good for that same reason. When I had woken that morning, my primary concern had been the church service. Were enough people going to come? Would enough of them bring food for the others? Had I assigned all the necessary roles? Were my words fitting for the occasion? The day had not yet ended, and to think that those were the concerns that filled my mind at its beginnings was a lesson in the surreal shifts of life. Unseen, unimagined, and always possible.

The hour was nearing midnight, or so I guessed, and the house was deathly quiet. I presumed my door was locked, but I did not check. What would be the point?

Lying down, I placed my head on the mattress and moved my arms from side to side behind my back, searching for some semblance of comfort, but there was little point in that either. That day had truly been long and yet I was not tired, at least not in any way I had ever known before, and so I lay in the darkened room, with my eyes covered and my wrists cuffed behind me, simply waiting for the answers.

How much I could see varied, but at that time, the blindfold was placed so it was open a sliver beneath each eye. I would look down and see the shadowed outline of my nose and cheeks, and then a morsel of the fuller picture beyond them. However limited this was, it still was something. That is the thing with sight. The most meager amount is a whole world more than none; and as that first blue light crept in beneath my door, I could see the morning stirring. Still no one came. Hours passed, and I sat waiting, quite unaware of whether I had slept in bursts or not at all, as a strange, hazy tiredness bore down on me. I shuffled along the mattress, sitting closer to the door, and strained to listen, but the house was soundless. Nothing, no people, no movement, no cars, nothing. Out of boredom, I lay down and then sat, and then lay down again, thinking of the questions I would ask them, thinking of my family, of how far the news of my abduction might have traveled, of someone telling my sisters in Gothenburg, Munich, and Cardiff, of my brothers in Iraq and Sweden, and of my mother. I tried not to think too long of her, afraid that the weight of it would be more than I could bear. When suddenly, a sound.

A key scratched at the lock, the handle twisted, and the door opened. The time I would guess was midday. One man walked in, and though I thought I felt the presence of another just outside the door, I could not say for certain. I was still sitting on the mattress when he reached behind my back and undid the cuffs, before placing a tray of food on the floor in front of me.

"Eat," he said.

"Why did you take me?" I began, but just as I had been rehearsing questions, he too had come prepared with a kind of answer.

"Not a word!" he said without hesitation. "You don't speak, and I don't know anything anyhow. We have no business in why. Eat. Tomorrow they will come, and they will talk to you. Eat."

Who will come? I wanted to ask, but it did not seem a wise idea.

Hearing him move off to the side, and the fact that he had undone my cuffs, gave me license to lift my blindfold a little. I did not remove it, but I made the opening wider to look down at the food he had brought. Water, a piece of bread, and a small plate of yogurt. I drank the water, but had very little of the rest. When I stopped eating for long enough for him to decide I had finished, he succinctly told me to bow my head and place my hands behind my back. Then, with the blindfold returned to its original position and the handcuffs securely locked once more, he took what remained of the food, closed the door, and left.

The rest of that day passed by without event. On three or so occasions my door would open and a guard would briefly enter. "Water?" he would offer, and I would hold out my hands to take the cup. I would drink it while he was there, and he would take it back before leaving. Nothing would be left with me.

Evening gave way to night, and a dreary tiredness caught up with me. The sediments of shock had settled in the stillness of that day, and the taut moments that had mined the depths of my energy, had left me feeling utterly drained and longing for sleep.

Come, Sleep! O Sleep, the certain knot of peace, the baiting-place of wit, the balm of woe, the poor man's wealth, the prisoner's release, th' indifferent judge between the high and low.

So goes the great Sir Philip Sidney poem, and if there was indeed release in sleep, then waking was renewed incarceration. I drifted off to the hazy world of dreams, and when I stirred and jolted awake, as I did many times inside the darkness of that night, it always took a few breathless seconds for me to decipher which was the dream and which the reality. I would open my eyes and still be unseeing, jerk free my arms and feel them still bound, until slowly, breath by breath, my confusion would settle, as the restriction and the pain in my body was proved too real for the dream to continue. *I am here. It is real.* I would count the people who had come to take me, and think about the things that had happened and the words that they had said. *I am here, and this is real. Be strong.*

At nearly seven the following morning, my door opened and two men entered. "Get up," the one man said, by which he meant for me to wake not to stand, but I was awake already. My eyes were open, though he would not know it because of the cloth that covered them.

They unbound my legs, kept my arms cuffed and the blindfold on, and led me out to speak to the men who had taken me.

CHAPTER 4

The Chair Man

By the gentle breeze that eased the heat from fast maturing, I imagined it was a pleasant and beautiful morning when they led me from the house where I had half slept those first two nights.

We needed no car for this brief journey. Just a few steps and twenty-odd meters before a hand pressed down on my shoulder, telling me to sit. They were very sparing in the words they spoke to me. Every sentence boiled down to the few words that mattered, to nothing more than the instruction. It was as though they all stood collective guard to a fragile secret code that I must not be given the meagerest chance of deciphering; and yet perhaps I give myself too much credit in that description, for once you strip away all traces of affection, issuing clear, non-negotiable instructions is not dissimilar to the way one may speak to a dog. The hand pressed down on my shoulder and so I sat, with my back leaning against what the touch of my fingers quickly recognized as the sturdy bark of a tree.

Through the tall grass I had seen, as they moved me from the back of one car to the boot of another, the rough bumps of the un-paved roads we had taken, and the length of that drive, combined with the present smell of plants and soil and the indistinguishable sounds of birds and insects, I was led to believe that I was sitting beneath a tree surrounded by acres of farmland. In time, my eyes would be opened, and I would know that to be true.

So much of it was waiting. For half an hour I sat alone and listened to the voices of many. They stood together somewhere in the distance. I could hear the sound of their footsteps, of the door opening and closing, of people moving around each other, of the unknown edges of unheard words, of the smeared sounds of expression. In the language that we shared from birth, they spoke of me, these people, in hushed tones they spoke of me, and I could not hear them. Birds muttered and flapped their wings, branches shook, the wind glided through the trees in a broken whistle, and I sat waiting.

When finally they came, they came together. With my legs crossed beneath me, my cuffed hands pressed to the bark, I straightened my back in preparation as I heard and felt them crowding in around me.

A chair was passed forward, the sound of its legs unmistakable as it was dragged through the dirt, settling a meter in front of me, on which a man lowered himself to sit.

Unseeing, I turned to him.

Out in the open space, I felt the walls close in and the air grow sparse, as for a slow minute they seemed content to merely study me up close in silence.

"Do you know why we took you?" asked the Chair Man quite suddenly. His voice was deep but free from the hoarseness of age.

"No, I don't," I sincerely answered. As I had barely spoken for these last two nights, the words tripped a little on exit, and I cleared my throat to steady my voice. "I think you have taken the wrong man."

"No," he replied, his tone slow and considered, exuding confidence and authority. "We well know whom we have taken."

"I am a priest in the church. . . ."

"And you think we don't know that?" he asked.

"Then what use do you have of me? I have nothing for you."

"You, like all of them, you all cooperate with the Americans."

"No," I shook my head and answered, "I have never dealt with Americans. I don't deal with them, and I have no dealings with them."

"Well, we will see," he said skeptically, "Inshallah [God willing], we will see."

Emboldened by the truth I had spoken, by the fact that I could not be rightfully accused of actively cooperating with the American army, I pressed on with the point. "Go ask the people," I suggested, my voice growing firmer with each word, "ask the people about the priest, ask them about me. About who I am, and when you go to ask, don't ask the Christians, go ask the Muslims, ask the *Muslims* about the priest of this area and see what they tell you about me."

"We have asked, and we will ask, and soon we will see," he said before pausing, and I could feel him looking at the others, I could feel them evaluating what I had said, and whether there was need for any further questions. "Do you want anything?" he finally added.

"I don't want anything," I answered. "I want you to let me go."

"We will," he said. "We just have something that must be done first, and then Inshallah, we will let you go."

With that, he stood up, and I heard them all walk off together, to leave me as I was beneath the tree. For some time, I remained there as they went back inside the house, no doubt to speak of me, and of that unsaid thing in need of doing.

An hour passed before the sounds of the outdoors were punctured by the footsteps and revving engines of those departing, after which, my guards returned and escorted me back to the small room and the mattress on the floor. Only this time, I would be able to see it, for soon after taking me there, the guard entered once again with a tray of food and a glass of water. On this occasion, however, after he unbound my hands, he did not stay in the room with me. "Eat," he had said, before I heard the door of the room close behind him.

Cautiously I lifted the blindfold, looking down and to the side so if he still happened to be in the room, then the only part of him I would see would be his foot. He was not there. Two days may not seem too lengthy a period, and when I look back at it now, in the great scheme of it all, it does not, yet they were the first days and the first of anything is different. My eyes ached as I opened them, and I was unsure whether the pain was real or was of my own making, an extension of the fear I felt from the sudden influx of light after so much darkness. Either way, there was little time to dwell on it. The guard would soon return, and he would take the light with him. Squinting, I ignored the food and looked about the little room that was my prison cell. It was disappointingly much as I had imagined. Sometimes you don't need your eyes to see.

It was small, I estimate fifteen feet in length and ten in width. The white tiles that covered the floor were in good condition and not overly filthy. In fact none of it was. Even the thin mattresses, of which there were three, were not torn though they were somewhat gray and dusty. In the far corner was an empty cabinet with its drawers partly opened in varying degrees. I stared at it, and a sad feeling crept over me. *This had been someone's house.* Someone's home, which these people had taken. I wondered what clothes had once filled those open drawers? A child's perhaps, and as I began to think of that, I thought of the echoes that move throughout this world without dissipating. Of a heavy stone falling in the vast and open ocean. Of the splash and then the ring of consequences that extends in all directions, passing through the endless mass of people who surround it. And as it does, as it sends them bobbing inside the waters, their arms begin to flail in a desperate bid to stay afloat. And thus the one large ring gives birth to a million others, which may appear smaller from above but are everything to those inside them. In this way, we are all connected, and it is wonderful and dangerous, marvelous and hideous, and I can't but worry. I worry that the effects of the hideous are far harder to halt. I worry that it takes only selfishness to stop the good from spreading, but to stop the bad, to stop the bad, you need forgiveness, and what could be harder than that?

I was near Torino, Italy, in a small village called San Chiaffredo, in the city of Cuneo, when, staring at the television, I watched as the second plane smashed into the World Trade Center. I cannot quite recall how I had filled the day before that moment. I doubt many can, but I would hazard a guess that most can remember the exact place they were when they saw it. It was my third year out of Iraq and the sixth of my studies for the priesthood. Much of my time then was dedicated to learning, and I was living with a number of other young men, each of a different nationality and all studying for the same purpose. Sitting in the living room, I called out to my friend Don Roberto as I watched in disbelief at the scene unfolding on the television in front of me. "Don Roberto, Don Roberto," I cried out, "come quick, something is happening in America, the world is turning upside down!" It is an expression Arabs often use. "The world is turning upside down" alludes to an unimaginable chaos. I doubt I had ever said it with more truth than I did just then. We both sat and watched, and I was sure that, though it was in itself a horror, it would mark the beginning of a series of disasters. "The Americans will not let this be," I said ominously to my friend, and I assume like most people, our minds then raced off to imagine what path the world had tilted to.

As snippets of information were revealed in the days that followed, a name known to many became known to all: Al Qaeda. The terrorist organization responsible for bombings and atrocities around the world, all perpetrated in the name of God and religion, had once again announced itself in the loudest way possible. It may seem strange to others, though it does not to me, that even as I dreaded what would befall the Arab and the Western worlds alike when infected by the all-too-familiar contagion of vengeance, I did not think of its effects specifically on Iraq. In my mind, this had little to do with Iraq. Not only was there not a single Iraqi among the hijackers, but Saddam Hussein himself had long been viewed as an enemy by the Jihadists. A secular leader, who did not govern the country in accordance with sharia law, and who murdered all who opposed him regardless of their faith.

However, blame began to travel in all manner of directions, and old rivalries, which had for a time been relegated to the backdrop, sprang back to the forefront of action. A terrible day that changed the paths of so many people in so many places. I have heard many arguments that surround it, with one harkening to the absurdity of the world in whole for the balance of empathy, and that is one I have often spun inside my mind.

Many died in America that day, but many more died in Iraq as a consequence. Many die today in many countries, and if we were to weigh the casualties of that day in some grotesque measure of tragedy, on the scale of lives lost it would not register so greatly. It is a delicate fact that often elicits strong reactions, and if one were to point to it, then one would be accused of all manner of wrongs, even of condoning the events by failing to acknowledge the true scope of the tragedy. However, that is not the point I am making. I only point to what is obvious but unseen, and, in doing so, tender a reason for it. A defense of what appears to be a lack of empathy on the parts of people who fail to mourn for those who do not share their birthplaces and ethnicities. And the excuse is in the sheer number of tragedies throughout the world. So much wrong fills the world we today inhabit, so great is the mass of injustice and brutality, that for the survival of our sanity, we must corrode, at least in part, our capacity for empathy. For if we were to truly mourn for every death, for every massacre, from Iraq to Nicaragua, and from Papua New Guinea to Nigeria, we would grow mad with grief. And yet I cannot but feel there is a madness in not grieving.

All the tragedies in the world create ripples, but the consequences when that rock was cast into the ocean were the greatest and most far reaching I had ever seen. And the years had passed by to find me as I was, sitting in a small room, peering at the empty open drawers, not wishing to eat, and still very much bobbing in the waters.

I would learn this more as time went on, that in the midst of dire circumstance we cling very hard to hope, watching for any event that might bring about a change in fortune.

The following day, my fourth, passed in monotony. I was left to sit inside my room and, except for a brief visit for food, which I was looking forward to more for the nourishment of my eyes than my body, little else happened. However, as the afternoon faded and the day was well into the evening hours, nine o'clock I would say at a guess, my door opened. I was sitting on the mattress with my back against the wall and was immediately alarmed at the unexpected visit.

"Stand," a man ordered, and so I did. He held me by the forearms, maintaining my balance as another unbound my legs. Then with a tug he led me forward. "Come," he ordered once again.

I walked blindly through the house, allowing myself to be led to some unknown destination. Perhaps it was the suddenness of these shifts, taking me all at once from idleness to movement, that sent my pulse on such a frenzy. It was not simply fear but a kind of stationary exertion, quite unlike the breathlessness of exercise and more draining.

As I walked steadily behind my captor, I took short, tight-lipped breaths as my heartbeats ran out ahead of me. A door opened. The air changed. We had moved outside. A few more steps and then there was the sound of keys rustling, car locks popping.

"Where are you taking me?" I asked. "Don't speak," came the usual answer. I was loaded into what we use to called a "peekup," which is a pickup truck with a flat back used primarily for transporting goods, merchandise, or equipment, but that was not where I was placed. Instead I was ushered into a narrow space, directly behind the two front seats.

They must be simply moving me, I thought, though since this was the first of the moves, I was still fearful. Thankfully, it was not a lengthy drive, and within fifteen or so minutes, I was taken not to a house but to a field.

After a short walk, my legs carrying me forward without conscious effort, suddenly my captors stopped. After they led me a little farther to the side, I was told to sit. "You are staying here," the man said matter-of-factly, as he tied my legs and left. Two others would watch me here, and though there would be a number of moves to come through the long episode of my abduction, this field would be the place to which I would most often return, and with one of my new guards, I would build a relationship as close to friendship as one can have in such circumstances.

CHAPTER 5

Abu Hamid

They had not spoken to me, my two new companions, and I did not endeavor to begin a conversation. Silently, one of them had moved my hands from behind my back to the front, where he bound them once again. In the midst of all that was happening, it was an unexpected kindness, and I nodded wearily in thanks, though I do not know if he noticed.

As nighttime came, and the darkness of the day mirrored that beneath my veil, a simple thin wool cover was handed to me, and I heard the two men lie down on the ground. I heard their waists and legs rubbing on the grass in search of comfort.

Without seeking warmth, I pulled tightly at the cover they had given me and lowered my head to the earth below, hoping to sleep away the next few hours in this place.

The air, though hot, was not unpleasant, and under different circumstances, the grand simplicity of lying here beneath the sky would have been most appealing. A dot on God's earth, surrounded by the glory of creation. I smiled at the thought, and a sudden gulp of emotion arose in me. My eyes welled up with tears, and I drew heavy breaths to steady them. It were as though the smile cracked the dam of all that I had been holding in. Hearing the sounds made by my captors, I breathed again to stop myself from weeping. From weeping, not only at a memory the air had brought, but at the smile that came from a sudden feeling of God's closeness.

When I was a boy, the summer months were for outdoor sleeping. The beds that we had brought inside over the winter would be returned to the rooftop of our home as the heat climbed higher. Children long for company, and a break from the norm; the rooftop sleeping gave us both, and it was something we all looked forward to.

Once we woke, the beds would be folded, remaining on the roof to be unfolded that same evening. My mother would go up an hour before, bucket in hand, and sprinkle the roof with cold water to make the air that little bit fresher for sleeping, and soon the family would follow. She would bring bowls of fresh fruit and vegetables, of apples, pears, and cucumbers for us to eat, and we would laugh and talk before sleeping. There were only two discomforts to the rooftop nights. The first and lesser of the two was the harshness of the sun returning. Though my father would arrange the beds to give us as much time as possible inside the shade, at some point the sun would inevitably find us. The other was the mosquitos. Some nights we slapped at ourselves constantly in defense, and still would wake up itching. However, these minor drawbacks paled beside the benefits, and though I slept on the rooftop many times when I was older, some things, some places and times, we will always see through our eyes as children.

"Allah O Akbar."

With the break of early dawn, my captors woke and I listened to the noise of their prayers. "Allah O Akbar." Not far from where I sat shackled, the two men knelt and prayed to God. "Allah O Akbar." Quietly I did the same.

"I am going to bathe," one said to the other. "Watch him." It is funny, but I have always been particular about cleanliness, quite possibly to a degree that others may find excessive. When I traveled, as I often did during the years of my studies, I always made doubly sure that my bedding was freshly cleaned, and would find it a struggle to sleep on anything that I found remotely dirty. I shower every morning, and my clothes are always washed and ironed, yet there I was, in the same shirt, vest, pants, socks, and trousers I had been wearing four days earlier, having been moved from place to place on the floors of cars, in sweltering conditions, and having slept in an abandoned room and out in an open field. A bath sounded most welcome.

"Filthy Christian," I would hear them say, and well, by then, I guess it was somewhat true.

Once the bathing and the prayers had ended, I was transported in the boot of the car back to the solitude of my room. That was the only time when I would be without company, as no matter what they were doing, when I was outside, a man was always left with me.

Going from the field to the house and back again became my routine for these first few days. With my eyes unseeing, it was difficult to tell if it was in fact always the same house. The car journeys felt longer on some occasions, but I could not know for sure, as when I lifted up the blindfold to look around a little, some rooms were different, but the place felt much the same. It was all a part of the confusion that comes when the simple details cease to matter as life dissolves to nothing but the essentials, to nothing but survival, and eventually to the thing that transcends it.

I was beginning to recognize and plan for the difficulties I had not previously thought of.

There were only two things I had asked for in the days I had been there. They were the only permissible requests. Water and the toilet. I would call for them on need, and once my requests were lodged, I would wait at the back of a long one-man queue. Two hours passed by very slowly on the third night before I was escorted out back on the short journey to relieve myself.

A bad state can almost always get worse. I knew it then, and I know it now with full certainty. So when my door was unlocked on the afternoon of my fifth day, and my lunch was delivered, the thought of being stranded to soil myself was a most effective suppressor of hunger. Bread, sauce, and potatoes. I ate a little and left the rest.

In the evening, I was taken in the furnace of the car boot to the orchard for sleeping. Another day gone and still no change, no advancement. I lay there on the ground, my captors close enough to touch, the sounds of their breaths beating like constant drips against my conscience. From beneath my veil, I looked upward to God and wondered *why?*

Have I not been good with you? Have I not done all that you had asked of me? Have I not helped my people at any time I could? Why this? Why would you put me here? Where is the reason?

I looked, all night I lay and looked, and I could not see it.

"Allah O Akbar." My eyelids felt heavy as I half lifted them to see a lighter shade of dark beneath my veil. I could not tell how long I had slept. My probing thoughts and questions were like stones skipping across the water without sinking, and only in the hiccup of the in between did I dip into a shallow rest. My energy was sapped and the dreariness of the days drained me further.

"Stand," the one man ordered.

I barely heard him.

"Sheep, stand!" he said, his hand gripping me beneath my shoulder.

With my arms cuffed behind my back, I rocked to the side and pushed myself upward, my balance almost eluding me. "Walk."

He led me forward, and I followed. Twenty meters and twenty minutes, back to the car and back to the room, I thought. Except when we arrived, and I was pulled out of the boot, gasping for air as always, I was not walked to the house and then to my room.

Strange that I half knew it without seeing, so quickly did I feel something was different. "Sit," said the hand pressing against my shoulder, and I lowered myself to the grass, my heartbeat quickening, all lethargy gone.

There was little waiting then. Footsteps. Seven pairs if I had to guess, and then the chair leg scratching, stopping in front of me.

"We have asked about you," the Chair Man said, his tone crisp and even, "and we heard good. They told us that you have no cooperation with the Americans."

"I told you I have no dealings with the Americans and never had!" It was the truth, and though there was no rational reason for it, a sudden anger rose up in me at having been doubted. "So what do you want from me?" I asked forcefully.

"We have something planned with you. Once it is done, then we will let you be," he calmly replied.

"And what is this thing you want, you want money?"

"No," he answered. "No, we don't want your money,"

"Then what? What is it you need from me," I pressed, searching desperately for some fragment of an answer.

"Not from you," he said. "What we want is a transaction, an exchange, you for another, one prisoner for another."

"What can you get for me?" I asked in all sincerity. "I am not the kind of prisoner that people will be looking to bargain for. I am a simple man, a man of peace, who helps all people, Christian and Muslim, as you asked and now know well."

"*A simple man?*" he repeated. "No, you are not a simple man! The world has turned upside down because of you. The ministers ask after you, the parliament asks about you. The president," he said pausing, "he spoke of you, he said *your name*, he asked for your release. *You* are not simple!"

My heart sank. I was filled with a hundred questions, and no words to express them. How complicated had this become?

"No one will touch you here," he said in reassurance. "God willing, we will soon finish our business and then release you."

Feeling myself grow very tired once again, I nodded slowly in acknowledgment.

"Is there something you want?" he asked. "Something you need?"

"Yes," I answered. "I want to wash. I want water and soap, if you would bring me that."

"Bring him a bucket of water, a bowl, and soap," he ordered of some faceless other. After he left, I was given the things I had asked for, along with jogging trousers and a new t-shirt. I stripped down to my underwear and washed myself slowly in the soap and water, not knowing when I would get the chance to wash again.

For the rest of that day and night, from the room and to the orchard, my mind swirled in thought at what the man had told me. I had been starved for any kind of information in a situation where the danger heightened my hunger for it. Where the downside of helplessness was so resoundingly apparent that I had been left with nothing but introspection, and every thought ended in a reminder of how little I knew and how little I could do about it. Thus that one conversation, which to the outsider may not seem revealing, especially considering its truthfulness could not be blindly trusted, was to me a banquet of details, and I sat hungrily pondering each one.

I pulled and pried at them, laid them out separated, and then assembled them back together, all on a bed of likely truth and likely meaning. Why would he lie? If he had told me that I was held for the purposes of ransom and not exchange, would it affect my very restricted behavior? What reason would he have to lie unless there was a task that I had not yet thought of, such as a phone call in which I would reassure others I was alive and well enough to be worth trading? "You are not simple," he had said almost in accusation, and the word continued to prickle me. Simple. Simple. The very thing that faded with each of his measured revelations.

I listed back the names, or titles, of those who had asked about me. The parliament. The ministers. The president. No doubt the church also, the patriarch, and of course my family, they who had also found themselves held captive to worry and hope.

If all this were true, as I did not doubt then that it was—after all, it did not take too grand a leap of faith to think that some attention would be drawn to the first priest to be kidnapped, in a place where every good and evil always comes with a religion that supposedly birthed it—then what price had these men assigned to me? When every plea for my release, every official who spoke on my behalf, served to increase the cost, and perhaps decrease the likelihood, of its happening. It is a perverse way to look at it, and yet from where I lay, sleeping on the grass beside my captors, my gratitude to the well meaning came second in importance to assessing the real and likely consequence.

I wondered who from the church was negotiating on my behalf, and with whom they were speaking? Had my family been contacted directly? What were they asking of them? Was it only for a prisoner exchange or were they negotiating for ransom?

Little of it was clear, and I had only time to ponder and guesses to make. Later, I would learn that there had been some truth to what the man had told me. Many people had spoken for me, all those he listed and more. The Italian ambassador, the president of Iraq, and even His Holiness, the pope, had asked and prayed for my release. Many people spoke on my behalf and prayed for my safe return, and that is something I will always be grateful for. What the man had, however, failed to mention was that negotiations were also ongoing for ransom, and both my family and the church had been contacted.

The increased price these men had come to attach to me was not entirely without benefit. "No one will touch you here," he had said, and I, being freshly struck with the sudden glimpse of the outside attention I had garnered, barely took note of these words or their value. I had become a rich commodity, and it seemed reasonable that they would therefore keep me undamaged, or as undamaged as a man could be in my situation. Those who stayed with me in the orchard, and those who guarded me from beyond the confines of my room, did not seem to be men of rank. Whenever I endeavored to speak to them, they quickly silenced me, and one of them had on an occasion bluntly said that, even if he were willing to listen to my questions, he had no information with which to answer them.

As the insects hummed their lullabies, and my captors drew deep sleepy breaths, I closed my eyes in the pitch dark night and hoped that such men as these would not dare to cause me harm without express authority. That I would be protected by my not being simple. However, the reality would turn out to be far different.

The day that followed, the seventh of my captivity, brought about a conversation that would begin the oddest friendship of my life.

Close your eyes for a lengthy while, and all sounds begin to rise in volume. The noises unstick themselves from one another, calling out their place and making distinct the many facets of their makeup. Voices are distinguished by pitch and crack and tempo, letters wrapped in the cadences of dialect, echoing wordless sentences of I am joyful, I am fearful, I am concerned, or I am excited. Sentences of I am harsh because I have to be, sentences of I truly hate you. More than this, though, is a feeling that gradually awakens, a meshing of all the senses—the sounds and the smells, the feel of grass and cloth and wind and heat, all the parts that make up the character of one's surroundings, of a time and place and of those who occupy it. I believe we all have that intuition, that foreign voice that is more ours than any other, always talking in a whisper, always guiding, warning, and informing. I believe we all have it, we all hear it. It's just not until your eyes are closed for a lengthy while that all sounds begin to rise in volume.

For a reason that I cannot explain fully, I had begun to think that, though many of my guards rotated, one particular man was around me daily, always in the orchard.

That afternoon, when I sat idly on a plot of shade beneath the sun, reflecting on everything and trying to think of as little as possible for a short, peaceful while, that one guard suddenly broke the quiet of my mind with a question.

"We saw that thing in your pocket," he said, and even though it was only the two us, it took a moment, and his repeating of the words, for me to realize that they were meant for me. "That computer thing in your pocket, that . . ."—he paused, I imagine to indicate its size with his hands, forgetting for a second that I could not see them—"blue thing, for the computer. Can I have it?"

When I was taken, they had removed whatever belongings I was carrying in my pockets. There were not many. A mobile phone; a wallet with IDs; a couple of notes; perhaps a coin or two of loose change if I happened to have any that day, which in truth was not so likely as the rate of inflation in Iraq after the Gulf War had brought coins to the border of extinction; a few sticks of Wrigley's spearmint gum, the last of the packets I had brought with me from my last trip to Wales to visit my sisters; and lastly a small blue memory stick.

I cleared my throat, struck by how utterly odd this very simple question was in the context of where we sat.

"Yes," I answered. "Yes, take it."

And that was it. He did not thank me but simply went back to whatever it was he was doing to occupy his time before that moment. And though I returned back to my contemplation, quietly my mind began to draw an image of a young man I had not seen. A young man who would ask permission before taking something from another, even if that other was his prisoner. In his question was a glimpse of innocence in a place where too many seemed guilty of too much, and the truth was I needed it.

The following afternoon, once the other guard had left the two of us alone, our conversation began again. Looking back, I suppose he had grown curious as to who this man was he sat guarding in the orchard every day, and so he asked me.

"You are a priest?"

"Yes," I answered. "I have a parish in the Dora, that was where they took me from."

He grew quiet, and I felt him nodding.

"Can I please have some water?" I requested. Without answering yes or no, he moved and a full cup was placed in my hand. I took a sip and ventured a question of my own.

"You," I said, "why are you doing this?"

I did not know for sure how he would reply, and I was still cautious not to upset him, to not overstep a line I could not see.

"I have nothing else to do," he quietly answered.

"Why have you nothing else to do? You are a worker or a student?"

"I am a student."

"A student where?"

"In the Institute of Technology in Al-Zafaraniyah," he proudly answered.

"Then why do you do this?" I asked again. In truth, I could not help it. Suddenly I was transported back to my former life, back to talking to one of my many pupils. "You are a student, do your studies, work. Is that not better for you than this?"

"No, that is not possible for me. We can't go there. Any time we go there, they will kill us!"

"Why not?" I asked. "There are many who go there."

"We can't go there," he repeated.

The university he had mentioned is in a Shiite area. If I still had any doubt about my abductors being Sunni, few now remained.

After a lull in this new conversation, and a period of silence, he spoke again, the words spilling out of him as though a thought in the corner of his mind had grown too fat to comfortably remain there. "I don't do what you think I do," he said.

"No?" I asked.

"No. I . . . mainly clean the guns. Hide and store them, here around the orchard."

There was little else for me to say, so I nodded, and I could not but ponder the unfairness of making quick judgments. On how the circumstances of birth can deal out impediments and advantages like playing cards to people who had no hand in choosing their seats at the card table. It is an inequality found not only in wealth and standard of living but in the maintenance of a good conscience, which for one may mean subduing his inner greed and for another may mean resisting what is expected of him in the normal circumstances that surround him daily.

For this young man, this current occupation was one of the few available to him, and he wanted me to understand, to see things from his perspective, and I did. I knew more about him than I had let on. I suspected that his name was Abu Hamid. I had heard it used on occasion, and I already knew that one of his principal duties was to clean the guns of the others. I knew it from the sound, a gift from my brief time in the Iraqi army.

In Saddam Hussein's Iraq, the law of conscription applied to all. Once a man completed his studies, he had to report for duty or else be deemed in breach and thus face probable imprisonment. In 1995, when I was twenty-three years of age, it was my turn to report. A law had recently been passed that permitted people, in times of peace, to pay a fee that would limit the terms of their service to three months of training, thus allowing them to avoid full deployment. The price was half a million Iraqi dinars, which at the time was equivalent to two thousand and some American dollars. It may sound like a paltry amount to pay, yet for us, it was significant. Being understandably less than enthusiastic about the prospect of spending much time in the army, however, I chose to pay the sum, which meant I had to fulfill only the non-negotiable training.

It is important for a man to learn his limitations as well as his strengths, and the three months away unveiled a shortcoming in me. I soon learned I lacked a talent essential for the smoothness of a conscript's time in training. I was terrible at bribery.

A few days before I was to leave, my brother Adnan, who is shrewder than I in all matters related to business, gave me a series of apparently simple instructions. He told me that there would be a sergeant in charge of my unit, and instructed me as follows:

> At times the sergeant will ask questions, such as who is good at fixing cars. Or who knows someone who supplies paper. It does not matter, because whatever it is he asks, I want you to put your hand up and say, I can help with that! You can then call us and we will take care of it. This is just the way it works. After you get them what they need, they will grant you a few days leave from service. Also, when you are alone with the sergeant, speak to him, ask if he has children. If he does, then we can bring them milk, sweets, or Pepsi Cola. Whatever it is he wants, you tell him you can help, and he will give you a few days off for it.

I nodded in agreement, but the idea never quite sat with me. I knew that it was harmless, but still it seemed sinful to engage in deceit to shirk my duties. So when I did arrive for training, and the sergeant asked his questions, just as my brother had said he would, I never put my hand up for anything that was not true, which meant that I did not put my hand up at all.

It was a difficult time. Though my sporting background served me well, the training was still more demanding than I had imagined it would be. It consisted of a lot of running and fitness work, as well as weapons proficiency and the operation and maintenance of a range of firearms. The days were long, and my incapability of procuring leave was proving troublesome. It was not until the second month, when I was left alone with my sergeant for a moment, that he, perhaps having recognized my deficiencies when it came to bargaining, turned to me quite abruptly and said, "I have very small children, you know, milk is always scarce in our house." "Of course," I said excitedly, "I can help with that!" That would be the one and only time I gained a few extra days of leave.

My skills in bribery were not improved by my brief time in the Iraqi army, but as I listened to the familiar sound of the guns being pulled apart and cleaned by Abu Hamid, I thought back to those days and remembered that even hard times have sweet moments.

CHAPTER 6

This is where we end them.

I am not a great believer in the justice of this world. That disbelief, if you will, is one of the lessons that comes when the knowledge gained from experience teaches us to unlearn the expectation of fairness we were born with.

Though I firmly believe in God and heaven, I likewise believe in understanding goodness and the need for it to be its own reward. I have seen too many bad actions propel people to high stations, too much greed feeding on itself in a climb to the kind of state the accumulators confuse with happiness. I have seen too much of all of that to ever believe fairness to be the law of this world and of this life. It is those who believe it to be who pin the blame for their disappointment on the tyranny of God, or on his lack of existence. I do, however, believe in cause and effect, and on my eighth night, as the darkness set once more and I lay my head down to sleep, the consequences of an old habit once again caught up with me in the most inconvenient of surroundings.

"Why don't you have some tea with your sugar?" would be the frequent joke as I piled teaspoons into the slender cup, which we call a "stican," before topping it off with dark brown tea. Ever since I was young, I have always had a sweet tooth. I consumed everything from desserts to sugary drinks with eager abandon. Unfortunately, the consequences of this habit have been a steady stream of tooth fillings and removals, root canals and crowns, and aches that often strike forcefully without warning. I cannot tell you why, but they seem to begin mostly when I am lying down, and am close to sleeping.

When my back tooth throbbed that night, and I felt the pain begin to jump beneath my eye, and then back to my tooth, my first thought was *please not now! Not here.* My hope and will and reason were like heavy books stacked high in my weary arms, and I needed all my strength to keep them balanced. This most inconvenient of additions was at the very least unwelcome. A severe toothache is one of the easiest pains to describe to people, because everyone at one time or another has felt it. No explanation is necessary. The mere mention of the word *toothache* is sufficient to jog the memory, to evoke the feeling of its spreading, of its being attached not to one place but to an area, of the side of one's face humming with a faint vibration. I moved my tongue in search of the offending tooth, and winced when I found it. I would later learn that the top gum on the left side of my mouth was infected, and that was the source of the pain. That night rolled by slowly, and I longed for the relief of sleep without ever achieving it.

The following morning, I waited patiently to be left with Abu Hamid. When, by early afternoon, the other guard uttered a brief goodbye and departed, I waited a little while more and then asked the young man for a favor.

"I need your help," I said, "I would like a small handful of salt please."

I had no food and the request seemed to confuse him for a moment.

"What do you want to do with it?" he asked.

"The salt, I need it, I need to put it on my teeth. My teeth are hurting me."

"Huh, ok," he said as he considered for a moment. "I can get you a little, but you don't say anything to anyone about it."

"I won't say anything. And also, if you can, get me some tablets of paracetamol."

"That is not easy," he said. "I will try."

I thanked him, and we spoke more in tiny bursts of conversation, always of minor things. An hour or two later, I was taken to a different place and then brought back in the evening. My movements were becoming more erratic and drawn out. Twenty-minute drives in the boot or the back of a car, and then back again. In truth, on such drives I rarely felt as though I were being taken to be killed or discarded; instead I reasoned that the movements were intended to reduce the chances of a military or police raid to liberate me. That was the way I thought in those first two weeks. Things would change soon after.

The following morning, true to his word, Abu Hamid came. In his hand he carried a torn piece of plastic bag containing half a handful of salt. He did not bring any tablets, but at least he had brought that, and so I used it. Perhaps a large part of the relief came from the act of doing, of administering what little medicine there was. Still, as I rubbed the salt from my finger onto my gums, I felt the pain quieten and subside.

During one of our talks, Abu Hamid had mentioned something that stuck in my mind. "The air is nice here," he had said, and I agreed. "It is because of the river." That was it. As always a small bit of information and nothing more. I did not ask for more, and he did not think to offer. Still it was another piece to the picture of where I was. Somewhere in the southwest of Baghdad, not too far from home. I can't recall the exact day he mentioned it, but I remember on the afternoon of the tenth, I got to hear the waters rush.

A group of men had come to the orchard. This was not wholly uncommon. There were other times when other men came, but as always I did not hear them well as they kept their distance from where I was sitting. However, on this occasion, we walked. My legs were at most times unbound when I was in the orchard, and with my wrists cuffed behind my back and my eyes covered as always, I was led across the fields alongside the others. If I had to guess, I would place the number of our group at six, including me.

The pain in my tooth was still troubling me, but this peculiar journey relegated it to a lower status in the list of things that occupied my attention. Walking is not so easy a task to the newly blind, and I strained to look downward through the sliver of an opening to steady myself. The direction was handled by Abu Hamid, who had placed his hand on my shoulder to steer me, but it was not long before the sound of the water would have been guidance enough. A piece of information that would prove vital to me on a day to come.

Once there, I sat and so did they, though not beside me. Quietly, I took in my new surroundings. The air and the water had become my outstretched hands, tapping on every obstacle they encountered, ringing out a multitude of sounds so I could see without looking. The grass below me was long and bristly, and, from the way the water sounded when hitting the edge, I imagined that tall plants and straw lined the banks of the river.

Time dripped on as I sat within my thoughts, listening to the sounds of nature and the echoing voices of my companions, when suddenly a different noise drew closer. Footsteps and the slap of sandals, closer and then beside me.

"You," he said, as though it were an accusation. "You will become a Muslim?"

I closed my eyes beneath my veil as I felt him hovering over me, waiting for the answer. For a second I dreamed that I was sitting beside myself, telling myself to breathe. To not fold in on the anger of the moment. The anger that was filling me. I was angry at the helplessness of the situation in which the world had placed me. I raged at all those who had set us on this course, at all those who had a hand in the destruction of my country. At all those men who hold God as a license for doing, a badge they possess that means all others are inferior to them, unworthy of life or dignity. A part of me was breaking, and it wished to howl against the wrongs that have no connection to reason, that grind against those who still dare to believe in humanity. I raged at that more than at anything else.

"No," I said, my head bowed as it shook from side to side, "no, I cannot."

"Why can you not?" he asked, leaning closer.

"Would you?" I answered. "Would you change? Would you allow yourself to abandon your religion and become a Christian?"

"No, but Islam is the true religion!" he shouted, and just as I could feel the water and the grass and the wind in the trees, I felt the poison of this man's hatred toward me. To kill me where I sat would have been a pleasure in his eyes, a righteous deed in a day well spent.

"My religion is also the true religion," I said. "Any man will tell you that his religion is the true religion. You say it and I say it too. Also, you invite me to Islam, and Islam says 'la ikraha fid deen.'"

Being a scholar of religion, I have studied the Koran extensively and in its pages it is written that no man can be forced or obligated under threat to become a Muslim, as that very threat invalidates the truth of his pledge, thus rendering it meaningless.

"How then can you ask me to become a Muslim?" I continued. "How can you ask me when I am under pressure, when I am under threat? Would my faith not then be untrue? Would it not then be a false statement?"

"No," he coldly answered. "Who is threatening you? No one is threatening you?"

"When I am free," I said, "I can think if I wish to be a Muslim and then my faith can be true, but now, here, it cannot be, and I will not be, because like you I love my religion, like you I *believe* in it. You would not become a Christian, and I will not become a Muslim."

He took that in, and I heard nothing for a moment but the water, and it was almost as though he could see me listening.

"What do you hear?" he asked, the words scraping on his teeth as he spoke them.

"I can hear the water running," I answered.

"Yes," he hissed, "here is where we end them," and with a sudden twist he placed his hand beneath my shoulder and jerked me forward. I scrambled to keep my balance, my legs looking for a semblance of stability, my bound arms unable to reach out to steady me, and still he pulled. And as he did, with every movement forward, the sound of the river rose in volume. By the time he stopped, after many dizzying seconds, I could feel the drops of moisture jumping onto my skin.

"You will not become a Muslim?" he barked.

"I cannot," I answered, and I heard the movement of his rifle. The clink of a hand on metal, the rub of a tightening grip, and then I felt it. A thud against the side of my skull, the barrel pressing against my temple, tilting my head to the side and still pressing, like a hungry animal readying to bite. This will be the end, I thought, and my heart drummed away in anticipation.

"You will not become a Muslim?" he repeated, and I could sense his finger tapping at the trigger.

"I cannot," I said once more.

"I tell you here," he said, working himself rabid, pressing the barrel harder against my temple, "your life or Islam? Your life or Islam?"

None of the others were moving. No one would interfere.

This is where I die, I thought, right here beside the river.

"What do you say?" he screamed.

"I say that I will not change my religion."

Just once more, the barrel pressed firmer before it drew away. "We will see," he said. "We will see."

He pulled me back a little and left me there as I closed my eyes and tried to piece my nerves back together. *Breathe. Breathe.*

The following day, quite unbeknown to me, a strange incident grew from this riverside encounter. An incident I would only hear of months later.

On the same street in Dora where my church was situated was a school and a pharmacy. The pharmacy was small, and it was often run by nuns from the local convent. They relied heavily on charity and would dispense medicine to those with prescriptions, often asking for little in return. Sister Caroline, a nun who had been working in Iraq for many years, and whom I knew well from my time there, was busy behind the counter on an ordinary afternoon. Except nothing was ordinary at that time in Dora. Tensions were increasing at a faster pace, and the divisions of religion and belief were more prevalent than they had been for many years. Of course, something else lurked in the thoughts of any Christian living there, that their priest was kidnapped and had not yet been heard from.

As Sister Caroline went about her business, cataloging the various medicines that had been delivered, she heard the bell above the door ring that informed her of a person's entrance. A man had walked in, dressed in traditional Arab clothes, with a thick mustache and short dark stubble. Sister Caroline would later tell me there was little to distinguish that particular man from any other in the area.

For a moment, he looked about the place. Glancing at the medicines that occupied the shelves, but without choosing any, he turned and approached the counter.

"I would like some medicine," he said.

"Yes?" Sister Caroline asked, wondering what medicine it was that the man required, and thinking that his reluctance to specify might have been owing to a lack of funds or to the sensitive nature of the ailment, and perhaps in part to her being a woman.

However, the man was not coy, and, but for his hesitation to elaborate, he did not show any signs of nerves. He stared back unblinking, sure and unafraid, and the next words he uttered would freeze the sister where she stood.

"I need some paracetamol," he said. "It is for your priest."

Your priest!

The sister said to me that in that instant the blood drained out of her, and she was lost for words or actions. Not knowing what to do, she could only focus on my well being. If I needed the medicine, for whatever reason, then she would give it. Sister

Caroline turned around, grabbed a square packet of paracetamol containing two, eight-table blocks, and handed it to the man who stood there waiting.

"Thank you," he said as he took it in his hand and turned to leave, but before he did, he stopped for a second longer. "He is brave," he said, "your priest. They tell him to become Muslim, and he says, "'I will not be Muslim.'" Perhaps that was his way of reassuring her, or else he thought it right that she should know, that she would be proud. Either way, he said those words, then left, and Sister Caroline could do little more than stand there, filled with dread for my safety.

The following morning, true to his word, Abu Hamid handed me an eight-table block of paracetamol. Though we were quite alone in the orchard, still his words were in a whisper, "Your medicine."

I ran my fingers along the plastic bulges, taking a quick count of the tablets, before I stuffed them into my pocket out of sight.

"Don't tell anyone," he reminded me.

"Of course not."

"If you do, they will kill me, and you too."

"I won't," I promised. "Thank you."

Such a grave risk for such a small action. This was far more than he had to do, and I was utterly grateful for it.

The pain had yet to disappear, and knowing that the medicine would be a tremendous help should have lifted my mood that morning, but the events of the late night that had preceded it were like a thick cloud through which shone no daylight.

I could not hope to know the exactness of the hour when the first screech of noise ripped across the sky. My head was pressed against my shoulder. The tooth had awoken as I tried to sleep, and the tightness of contact served to steady it. That's the funny thing about sleep. I often do not think it will ever come, and then it does and I fail to notice it. I was asleep when the noise rang out, the sound of the air screaming.

"Allah O Akbar!" one of my captors bellowed in celebration. "Allah O Akbar!" and then that noise again.

I bolted upright where I sat, at once afraid and bewildered.

"Allah O Akbar!" he shouted again, as the air shrieked in those awful seconds before the thud of an explosion. It was the sounds of rockets being fired across the river, from our side to that of the Americans. *Our side*. What a dreadful thing it was to be one with these people.

This was the first of them, but it would not be the last. At other times, on other days, always beneath the shadow of the night, this horror of a rising war would rage beside me, chasing me out of whatever dream my mind had drifted into. With every screech and crash, I would feel myself shaking beyond control as I willed myself to be elsewhere. A hysteria would fall over me. *How will I ever leave this place?* I would wonder. Who are these people who hold me? No negotiation, no exchange, and no payment would ever save me. I was becoming more and more certain of it. This was the place where I would die.

Those two incidents show how the pendulum could swing from one extreme to another during my abduction, because it wasn't all bad, not in the mind anyhow. Sometimes I would scale the walls of horror, plant my feet on the bricks of fear and helpless desperation, only to find air and pure elation. It is a curious thing to live with death so close. To lose your sense of the banality of things, and experience nothing but extremes. To vault from loss to victory, from tragedy to meaning. When the rockets sounded overhead, I would fall inside myself, into a deep and empty well of darkness, but there were other times, the times when I held true to my God and my religion, when I would not give up myself for the sake of survival. That's the irony of it really—the pressure to kill who you are to stop yourself from dying. And every time I held on to myself, every time my grip stayed sure and strong, I felt the joy and power of true purpose. The purpose that began so long ago and carried me in these moments.

Fear is not always a bad thing. It can be like the ache of exercise, a pleasant sign of exertion. So much depends on the kind you encounter.

For me, in 1998, it was the most common of fears, that of the unknown and of failure.

I had completed my theology studies at Babel College, coming first in my class. The rector, Yousuf Habbi, a man who had much influence on my life and whom I admired greatly, pushed hard for me to be sent to Rome to further my studies. His efforts proved fruitful, and I, along with a fellow aspiring priest by the name of Firas Ghazi, was selected for the trip.

It was the first time I had left Iraq and, in knowing the difficulty of the studies I would be facing, I felt a great apprehension at the prospect of doing so. Yet that is the thing with the fear of failure. When considered in the quiet of reason, if the argument against doing boils down to nothing more than fear, then fear is never worthy of much merit. So I went. A car journey to Jordan. A plane ride to Rome. And then on to the historic city of Urbino, where the other students had been for two weeks before our arrival, busily immersing themselves in the Italian language.

If our delay were not enough, it became rapidly apparent that we were the least equipped of the students, and were much further behind our new colleagues than the two-week delay would suggest. Though my Arabic was undoubtedly strong, the only other useful language I knew was English, and my proficiency in it was more than a little limited. Around me, others, such as a Nigerian priest I met in my first week of study, spoke English and French with utter fluency.

These were the first real obstacles I remember encountering, when the road ahead seemed long and steep and it was *genuinely* hard to convince myself that I was equal to it.

Our time in this city, and in the village where we were situated before returning to Rome, was dedicated completely to improving our grasp of the language. After all, our proper studies would all be in Italian.

The place was inexpressibly beautiful, and the people most welcoming. Faced with time constraints, we all dove headfirst into our studies. When not reading, we were practicing the language, with the teachers, with one another, and with the local people. On my walks around the village, especially on Sunday after mass, I would endeavor to start conversations with the locals, and their openness to helping me left a very positive impression that has never faded. It is fair to say that I fell very quickly in love with Italy. I was thankful to God that this path he had placed before me had led to such a wondrous place, where I was growing both in knowledge and experience.

Once our time in Urbino ended, I went to the Vatican, and thus began my real studies. If studying Italian had been difficult, then studying the intricacies of theology in a language I did not understand was doubly so. But I was determined and joyful at having the chance. It was amazing to me to encounter so much beauty at one time. The church of St. Peter, the villas, the designs, the narrow cobbled streets. I was mad with it. How different it all was from Iraq, the heritage, the saints, the paintings. I could feel myself changing, and just as I was being reborn, I became like a child, thirsty to see, thirsty to learn—to learn how all this came to be, to know these people. Thirsty to discover how this beauty was created. What knowledge had made it happen.

Still, in that first year I struggled. Though I ventured out in the evening for extra Italian classes, when my theology lessons began, I could not comprehend more than 40 percent of their content. Having to constantly stop and check the meaning of words slowed me down tremendously, and my grades suffered as a result. I remained determined, however. This was the life I had chosen, and I would not fail at it. I would return from the evening lessons, take my Walkman, and climb onto the roof, where I would watch the nighttime views, listen to my cassettes, and practice my pronunciation in solitude. Otherwise, I would watch Hollywood movies in Italian. This helped me because many of these films I had seen before, often more than once. My favorite actor is Denzel Washington, and it was rare for me to miss one of his films, though if I were to pick a favorite movie from those I watched in Italy, it would have to be *The Green Mile*. Even now, if I am clicking through the channels and it happens to be on, whether it is just starting or is nearly over, I always stop to watch it.

Not being with my parents was an added difficulty. They had been with me all my life, even when I was busy studying far from home. Even in the isolation of the priesthood, when a daytrip was not permitted, as it was not during certain periods, still, they were close, and I felt their closeness.

Italy was a different world, which even its unique beauty highlighted the distance between it and that other to which I was accustomed, that other world where my loved ones dwelt. I would call them often, and they would always encourage me. My mother would worry, as mothers always do, and reassure me. My father, who held education in great reverence, would reaffirm the need for it. Now that may seem a simple thing, a given, but we grow quickly conditioned to our surroundings, and a glimpse of a differing perspective, even for an instant, can wake us with a clap to the greatness of our reality. He would ask me of my studies, he would tell me to work hard at them, and I would be reminded of the privilege of the chance I had been given. And knowing that, which is true of so many things, is a source of strength that keeps on giving. To feel that we are privileged, in the life and love we have, humbles us to work and work happily.

By the second year, my Italian had grown far stronger. I was comprehending, if not all, then 90 percent of my studies. Once again, though this time in the better sense, my grades began to mirror my understanding of the language. I had overcome my obstacles, forged new friendships, and was feeling quite at home. All was going well until a message on the twenty-second of July 1999 broke me without warning.

In the summer months, we were sent out to stay in Italian parishes, where we would have more opportunity to practice the language with the people. On that day, I was in Torino, in the north of Italy. The rector had phoned the parish priest telling him that there was news from Iraq, and that afternoon I was called to his office. I do not remember how he said it, if he asked me to sit down, if he led into the news with some other words. All I remember is the message. My father was dead.

I have been the deliverer of bad news before, and I have seen the way that people take it. Some become still, unmoved in a wash of shock. They grow small and fragile beneath the weight of it. You almost become tempted to repeat the words to them, as though they had not heard you, but you know they did. Others immediately ask questions, needing more details as though to verify the truth of what they had heard. Me, I was neither still nor inquisitive. I simply wept and wept and wept. Even the parish priest was taken aback by the unbridled manner in which my emotions overtook me. I was crying without breath or control, as though the minutes could not hold the volume of my tears. Sadness is far too small a word for such moments.

He had left without me seeing him, without me ever saying goodbye. The thought of it wracked me with guilt. I could not but feel that I had fallen short, and to this day this feeling lingers with me, a scar unseen but very present. He was my father, and I had not given him his worth.

My first thought was to return, to be there for his funeral, but that was not without its complications. Owing to the rules of conscription, and the country's no longer being in peacetime, returning meant the government could easily see fit to take me to the army, and I would lose the chance to complete my studies. Still, I wanted to go. It was more than a duty. However, all the family united in dissuading me from returning. So instead, I left for Cardiff to stay with my sisters Aida and Maysoon. There we grieved together as people do. We prayed and told stories of what he was like, and who he was to us. It was a sad summer, but in time my grief subsided. I hoped instead to meet him once again in heaven, and held on tight to our final conversation.

I was talking to my mother, when he briefly took the phone to speak to me.

"I love you," he said. "How are you?"

"I love you too," I answered. "I am good, I am doing well, learning a lot."

"Study hard."

"For sure. You know me."

"Yes," he said, "I know." And that was it. Three weeks later he was gone. *Study hard*, he had told me, and so I did, with relentless vigor.

In 2001, two years after my father had passed away, three of my colleagues and I were officially ordained as priests. Among them was Father Ragheed Ganni—an extraordinarily brave man, who would later return to Iraq with me, where he would become a martyr, shot outside his church by an extremist for refusing to close it. On a Sunday in 2007, when a man holding a machine gun asked him why, after being warned, the church had remained open, Father Ganni replied, "How could I ever close the house of God?" And for that, they killed him. I feel truly blessed for having known him.

Though I had become a priest, along with my three colleagues, my studies were not yet over, and after much work and continued effort, in 2003, I finally earned my master's degree in philosophy. Little did I know at the time that some three years later, the title of my dissertation would serve as my proof of life.

CHAPTER 7

A Good Man and the Americans

I missed so many things in those first days and the ones that followed. That is something people do not think about much when
they hear stories like mine. When they imagine themselves in a
position somewhat like the one I lived. There is so much imposed
upon you when the foundations of your life are shaken that your
thoughts are consumed with holding the wobbling stones in place,
with ducking out of the path of the ones that fall, with curling
tight for cover and standing tall to fight, all of that leaves little
room for people to imagine what it is they would miss in the idle
moments.

Habits are often confused with repetition, and though repetition does have something to do with them, it is not a sameness,
for to repeat something does not mean that it will be performed
identically.

A priest cannot do without giving mass. It was the habit for
which I spent years in training, and to me it is far more than
reading from a book or reciting from memory. It is the time to
soothe, to celebrate, and to inspire, to pass on the message of
God not only as it was originally written but as it matters now
and always. In the quiet of my room, I would write and rewrite

the words of my sermons. I would think of the issues of the day, of the fears felt and worries harbored, and of all the questions that they bring. From there I would aim to suit the answers to the questions. Beyond the assistance that I provided, both to my parishioners and to the priests studying at the college where I had taught, the mass was the basis of my purpose. By the fifteenth day, I missed it terribly. I missed the quietness of a church in prayer.

Here the questions to be answered were all my own. The hardship of my circumstance had made me both the parishioner and the priest, and yet by their very definition neither can exist without the other. My faith in God surrounded me, and I searched the volumes of my memory for answers. Every day I would recount another.

I cannot say each question answered was not asked again. That is not the way it works with these types of questions. Their answers are not quantified in calculable proofs. You cannot check off the answer once and for all. In these questions there is no end for you to find but the end that finds you.

The words were not spoken aloud. There was no sound but the faint pop of my lips parting. I bowed my head, closed my eyes beneath the blindfold that covered them, and spoke the lines inside myself and outward. These were a different set of seconds than before, time disintegrating and flowing in unison, invisible sand falling unseen and unending.

"The Lord is my light and my salvation," I would utter and repeat. "The Lord is my light and my salvation, whom should I fear?"

The first line twice, then ask the question.

The Lord is the strength of my life. The Lord is the strength of my life, of whom shall I be afraid?

I would speak the words and feel a strange and familiar comfort pass over me, in which I might see the outline of purpose in my suffering and in my probable death.

Blessed are the peacemakers for they will be called the sons of God. Blessed are those who are persecuted because of righteous-

ness; for theirs is the kingdom of heaven. Blessed are you when people insult you, persecute you and say all kinds of evil against you because of me.

My fear had not dissipated. I still felt it at times rise and choke me. When the gun was to my head, when the rockets fired in the dead of night, when I was bundled into the boot of a car, and the drive lingered, fear would inevitably find me. And yet in these words lay a challenge for me. For my faith, for my belief in Christ and in God. Much like my captors, in the morning I would pray, spending the remainder of the day in thought and contemplation. Over and over again, I would ask what was happening to me. What was the reason and the meaning of it and what was I being called to do?

In truth, I had no expectation of a sign and had yet to comprehend the full meaning of the challenge and what it would teach me. At times, I would think this was an invitation to martyrdom. Many men and women had died for our belief, both in this conflict and in all those that had preceded it. I cannot say that the thought did not trouble me. I had held on to my nerve on the few times I was closely tested, when death was a most realistic conclusion to my keeping to my belief, and still I feared being tested once more, and who I would be in the face of it. That was the challenge as I saw it then, and I would not see the rest as a whole until later. The only sign I felt I would find would be in my death or survival. My faith did not ensure that I would be rescued but that God would be with me no matter the conclusion. And in preparation for the possibility that the conclusion would be death, I prayed for my willful surrender to it. If my abduction were meant to end in death, as I presumed it would, then I would be ready for it.

Those were the first two weeks of my abduction. After that time, things began to alter.

I was sitting outside in the orchard with Abu Hamid on the fifteenth day when they came for me.

My legs were loose, my arms bound, and my eyes covered, as always. The day was hot, and the afternoon was drawing past its prime. It had been some time since I had bathed, and I felt the sweat sticking to me as I slowly cooked beneath the sun, my body itching with it and the numerous insect bites that seemed to cover me all over.

It was just the two of us that afternoon, and we had not spoken much beyond the odd word here and there. I was sitting some yards away in the usual doldrum of my thoughts, while Abu Hamid busied himself with whatever it was he was doing. The sound of him suddenly standing was the first noise I heard when the three men came to take me.

"Al Salaam Alaikum" (peace be upon you), one of them said as they drew closer, to which Abu Hamid replied, "Allah bil Khair" (may God bless you), a common form of greeting, which all the others echoed. From that point, I couldn't understand with any certainty the words exchanged between them, and there were not many in any case. Briefly they spoke to one another in hushed and jumbled sounds before the visitors approached me.

"Get up," the one man said. "Stand."

When there is little safety to be had, the sum of all there is rests in the narrow norms of an abnormal situation. I had been moved many times before, but never at this hour, and the difference alarmed me.

Placing my hands on the ground, I wearily stood up. The lack of food had transformed simple movements to laborious activities, and I gave my head a gentle shake to break the cobwebs of dizziness. Pulling at the chain, the man unlocked my hands from the front, only to cuff them once again behind me.

"Walk," he ordered, giving my shoulder a shove, and so I did. This part was as expected, the regular steps to the car that sat waiting, but waiting to take me where, I wondered. As its doors clicked open, and I moved to enter, the urge to speak reared up and I suddenly stopped to ask, "Where are you taking me?"

"What? You don't want to leave?" one of the men replied without a hint of humor.

"Of course," I answered, and as a second passed in silence, I felt the twitch of hope inside me.

"We will exchange you," said the man. "We will take you to the place where we will exchange you."

With his words still hanging in the air, a pair of hands aided and maneuvered me into the space behind the front seats of the pickup truck. I lay there for the remainder of the journey, contemplating the many questions I wished to ask and the miniscule chance of acquiring any answers.

By my estimate, the drive stretched near enough to the hour mark. Every time the car slowed down, as it often did, I thought we were perhaps arriving at our destination, but soon enough it would speed up again.

Conscience of my presence, no doubt, they barely said a word for the entire journey. With my arms behind my back, I was face down on the car floor, which was filled with dirt from the many boots that had trod on it. Jagged grains of mud and tiny stones kept pressing at my lips and cheeks as my head bobbed above the uneven road, and I remained unmoving in concentration. From one dirt path onto another, the car negotiated narrow bends, lurching and dipping while I lay quietly weighing the possibilities.

It could be true, I thought. Maybe this is the start of the end of it. If there were really to be an exchange, surely it would not be done near the place where they had kept me for all this time. No, I would be moved a safe enough distance away from the place they would return to, and there they might release me. *It could be true,* I told myself again, and then quickly cursed myself for thinking it. What use was there in that? Only disappointment. Far better for me to keep to what was true and likely. There would be no exchange for me. No prisoners released to these types of men, men who would think nothing of repeating the process. *Still, God willing, maybe.*

As the car eventually eased to a slower pace for too long a time for it not to have reached its destination, I felt my breaths grow fast and heavy and uncontrolled. Turning my head, I freed my mouth from the dusty carpet, but the air felt thick as I struggled for it. It was worry sliding back to fear.

The gear shifted. The engine revved down. The key turned. The machine quieted. The doors opened, and the men shimmied and shuffled out, their feet landing on the ground below.

One reached in and pulled me by the wrist. The other pushed from the opposite side, and I snaked back a little before rising. At times they had referred to me as the "merchandise," and at others, the "sheep," and these moves from place to place were much like transporting livestock.

I presume that the psychology of such name calling is to dehumanize the victim, to put him or her beyond the reach of empathy. Doing what needs to be done, free from the hindrance of considering the rights and wrongs of your actions. I presume that a psychologist would view it in this way, but I see it differently. The majority of these men would have had far more sympathy for me if I truly had been a sheep, incapable of being Muslim, much less of choosing Christianity. It is pleasant to think that everyone might be misunderstood, and that reason can always find the way to peaceful and respectful coexistence. That may be true for many, but it most assuredly is not for many others, and it is not because their faith in God is too strong. That is not the stick by which to measure. Rather, the prejudice that views those who lack a shared faith as inferior has sunk bone deep, through lengthy immersion in a lifestyle, through others having bred it from the start into your psyche, or through wrongs committed that cannot be undone. What all of these circumstances yield is the perception there is one truth that is unequivocal in nature.

In the hour or so that we drove, the afternoon had given way to early evening. There are differing shades to black. Different levels and darknesses. I do not know if this is simply my perception or if it is in fact true. Perhaps black, and maybe white also, are the only colors that do not differ in degree, and if we ever think they do, then it is only because we do not know the name of that other color that seems a shade darker or lighter. Beneath my veil, I saw a black that was not fully formed, and by that, and by the high-pitched sounds that rang out as we walked toward the house door that had just opened, and no doubt toward the man who stood outside of it, I knew it to be evening. The chirping birds had gone, to be replaced by the clittering of nighttime insects.

Past one room, down a short corridor, my left shoulder moved across my body, a right turn, enter, and a downward push onto a thin mattress on the floor, where I sat, back to the wall. My room. The door closed.

I heard them walking back along the steps I had taken, where they settled and talked a while. As always, I listened to the sounds of words, and no words in particular. This carried on for not so long. Close to a half hour. I guess they had to leave before it got too late. They moved, the door opened, and it stayed that way for a minute. Beyond was the faint noise of a car starting, wheels turning. Then the noise was gone and the door closed. I wondered what would come next and hoped that it would be different. That I would be told what would be done to me and what I was to do. A plan. A procedure. A time and date in the not too distant future. I sat and waited, hoping for much and expecting very little.

Some indiscriminate length of time then passed as I sat waiting. It seemed to me now that the man outside was waiting too. Then slowly, the door to my room cracked open.

I heard the footsteps move and settle a meter or so in front of me. The sound of a palm rubbing on cloth as the person knelt to face me.

"What is your name?" he asked, his voice a little gruff and unmistakably Iraqi.

"Saad Sirop Hanna," I replied, one name at a time, as clearly as I could say it.

"What is your work?"

"I am a man of religion. A Christian," I answer.

"Yes," he said, and there was a strangeness to the way he said it. "Yes," he repeated, as though he were confirming a fact he knew already.

The next words I was moved to utter were of my situation. Instinctively, I wanted to tell him that I had been taken. I guess it was because I wanted to say it so much to anyone that for a second I forgot the absurdity of spelling out what my appearance was screaming. Instead I remained quiet. Waiting for what he would do, and what he did was reach over to lift my blindfold.

I flinched at the touch of his hands, and even when the cloth was gone, still I was confused as to what he had actually done and why he had done it. My eyes opened gingerly, protesting against the sudden gush of light that struck them. Watery shapes gradually became recognizable as my legs, clad in old blue jogging bottoms, and as the thin gray-and-white mattress beneath them. Slowly, and still squinting, I saw; but I would not raise my head, I would not look at the man who knelt so very close in front of me.

"Open his hands," he told his son, who took the key from his father, and after some fumbling, turned it in the lock to pop the metal bracelet open.

"This is your home. I have nothing with you," the father said, leaning his head down so I could look at him, "and now, I will call the Americans to come get you."

Take any length of time. Whether it is a life in full or an episode within it. Whether it is dull and flat, or crammed with more troughs and peaks than your heart has strength to remember, and still you will find moments that break off from the rest.

"What?" I asked in utter disbelief, my eyes still low, still squinting.

"They are looking for you," he said.

"Who is looking for me?"

"Them. The Americans. I will call them."

I had prepared myself for many things before my door pushed open, but not for this. It had to be a trick. A test to see if I truly had ties to the American forces. To expose what was not there by somehow manufacturing it. Of course I would jump at the chance of rescue, and I could then be accused of colluding with the enemy. As though I did not have enough enemies where I sat. And yet, what if was true? What if he really wished to help me? My head throbbed with desperate confusion, and I knew not where to turn.

"I don't know these Americans you speak of," I finally said. "I don't know any Americans."

"No, don't be afraid," he reassured me. "Don't you want to leave?"

"I want to leave," I answered, the fluctuation in my voice betraying the truth of my annoyance at being once again asked that question, as though it were my decision. "I want to leave, but they told me, they said how it would happen. They said they are negotiating an exchange. That . . . that they were going to exchange me."

"Don't be afraid," he repeated. "Now I will call the Americans, and they will come for you."

Calmly, he reached across to help me stand, and for the first time I raised my head and looked at him. Late forties to early fifties, he had a thick, black moustache and a full head of hair, graying at the top and more so at the sides. Six feet in height and sturdily built, he wore a white dishdasha, the traditional Arab attire, and walked with a slight limp that hinted at a prior injury. It was that and the way he spoke, in a tone exuding authority, with each word precise and measured, that led me to quickly believe him to be a serviceman. A high-ranking soldier no doubt in Saddam Hussein's now disbanded army. His name was Ali.

That was my impression, and that is the thing; it is hard to know a man by how he looks and what he wears. What do bad and good men look like? Stand him beside my captors, and he could be one of them, and I still suspected that he might be.

We walked to the living room, and I subtly glanced about the place to find my bearings. It was a rural house, well constructed but very simple, with a kitchen, the room where I was kept, and the one in which I was then standing. The traditional sitting room for Arabs, wide and long with no furniture and thin mattresses tightly arranged from one end to the other, stretching across the entire floor.

"Sit, please," he said, before turning to his son, a boy in his early teens. "Tell your mother to bring some tea. Do you want anything else?" he asked.

"Water."

"Water also."

The boy nodded, walked off to the kitchen, then returned and sat beside us.

"Why did they take you?" asked Ali.

"Believe me, I do not know," I answered. "They took me from the church, from outside the church, and I don't know why they did it."

"Hmm. . . ." With every answer I would give, his eyes would momentarily narrow as he silently considered it.

"There are prisoner exchanges," he said, with a tilt of his head, as though perhaps that is the reason, that I was right about my earlier assertions.

"But this is wrong. I am an Iraqi like you, how do you do this?" I asked, aware of myself straying into dangerous territory, and likewise gauging his reaction.

"When did they take you?"

"Two weeks ago. Tuesday."

I heard the clink of glasses and a woman walked in with a tray in hand. On it was a small metal pot, three small tea glasses, a bowl of sugar, and three cups of water. She wore a headdress, but her face was showing.

"Thank you," I said, as she set the tray before the three of us. Quietly, she nodded in reply. A young child, dressed in turquoise pajamas then came running in behind her, and she quickly grabbed him so he wouldn't tumble into the hot drinks she had made us.

Ali began to pour the tea, while his wife picked up the boy, who flailed his arms in resistance. Out of the corner of my eye, I could see her walking back toward the kitchen, the boy held tight to her chest, when suddenly she stopped and turned back to her husband.

"Is this not sinful?" she asked, her free hand waving in exasperation, "is this not sinful? Why are they doing this to them? These are educated people."

"Yes," Ali nodded, as he handed me the thin tea glass, and I could not tell how convinced he was of her protestations.

"By God it is sinful! They are taking these people and destroying the country," she said in conclusion, before disappearing around the corner. I piled a spoonful of sugar into my tea, took a sip, and felt a little better at her show of empathy. Not just for myself but for all of us.

For the next minutes we sat and drank in silence, and all I could think of was the call he had promised to make. The Americans. Why had he not yet made it? The words of his wife had added a measure of weight to the truth of his intentions, but not enough for me to request the call. I still did not know whether I would speak if asked to. They had all lied to me. Could they truly have placed me in the hands of a man who would so readily hand me over?

When we finished our drinks, and his son took the tray away, leaving the two of us alone, I thought I would venture proposing a differing route of action.

"You seem like a man who fears God," I tentatively said, "like a man who does not desire to hurt people. I am here. What do I have to do with any of you? Why don't you help me? And I am ready." In other words, I am ready to compensate you. It was a big risk on my part to put this agreement on the table, yet it was one that would be expected from a prisoner, and if this were all indeed a trick, then this would be a far more forgivable offence then conspiring with the American army.

"I can't," he quickly said, and his lips tightened, as though the thought of it tasted bitter in his mouth. "They would kill me, and they would come and kill my boys."

"You don't have to help me escape, just let me run. . . ." I had begun to say, when suddenly a knock at the door froze me back to silence.

"Don't be afraid," he said, as he stood and pulled the door ajar. "He is my brother. We will look after you."

Even with all the turbulence of that time, this was a most peculiar situation to be in. I thus far had had few decisions to make. There had been little choice to any of it. Sit. Stand. Be quiet. At the odd times when I was asked a question, the truth was all I had had to return in answer. This was the first time that I had a real option, and I felt myself at the end of a pendulum swinging between comfort and dread.

The brother stepped a meter or so into the room and hastily closed the door behind him. That was where he stayed, and as the two of them spoke, he stared at me as though I were a bomb capable of exploding at any instant. He was the younger of the two, by ten years or so, but they were unmistakably related. Perhaps that was why I imagined he too was an army man of sorts.

"You cannot do anything for him," said the brother. His voice was a little hushed but loud enough for anyone in the room to hear.

"We can make the call and try," insisted Ali.

"This man. It is very dangerous." He did not need to complete the sentence for us all to know it. No part of this was safe, and Ali shook his head in resignation to that fact. Either way, their minds were made up, and there was little point in talking. They came and sat beside me, and as I remained quietly waiting for the verdict, Ali reached into his pocket and drew out a small, black mobile phone. He began to dial, and my heart began leaping.

I wanted to take another drink of water, but I could not move from the spot on which I sat, my fingers nervously scratching at the marks on my wrists where the skin had chafed from the constant rubbing of metal.

"This is Ali," he said in English, his accent thick, rolling out the words on jagged edges, "yes . . . yes . . . I have the priest . . . the priest . . . the one you looking for . . . yes . . . they bring him here."

Straining, I could hear what sounded like an American on the other end, faint and barely audible. This was too much trouble for a trick, I thought, and I could barely stop myself from shaking.

"Yes, I have him here," said Ali. "Here," he repeated, trying to convince the man on the other end that he was not lying. "He is with me . . . now. He can talk to you."

He extended the phone to me, and what else was I to do but take it? I put it to my ear and could hear the swoosh of an open line, but no voice was on the other end. Stalling for agonizing seconds, I willed the man on the other end to speak first and confirm that he was indeed whom I hoped he would be, but he too remained silent, until I could not keep silent any longer.

"My name is Saad Sirop Hanna. I am a parish priest. I was kidnapped fifteen days ago, and I am with Mr. Ali. Please come and get me!"

"Ok, understood," replied an American voice on the other end. "Give me Ali."

Goodness is an invisible substance. You really cannot tell its strength until it's tested, until enough of life is piled on it, and you can hear it creak with the weight of temptation. The temptation to forgo what can be done in exchange for the ease of not doing. Perhaps it is only in the direst of circumstances when true goodness can find its measure.

CHAPTER 8

Ibn Rushd

A few hours earlier, he had returned to me my sight, and I had not dared to look at him. As Ali folded the phone and tucked it back in his pocket, I studied his face for clues to the outcome.

"He has to speak to his people," he said. "Tomorrow we call them, and they will tell us what to do."

The news was good. My liberation, which had seemed to be becoming a decreasingly likely possibility, had in one phone call become a probable outcome. However, there still lingered that familiar uneasiness around us. Nothing is simple in the places where war and hate and greed are pulling from all directions. Life there is too complex for dreaming of ever afters.

His children came. There were three in all. The young man who uncuffed my hands and another two: a boy and a girl, who appeared to be so close in age and appearance that they could well be twins. I did not ask for confirmation, but that is the way I think of them now, when something sends me packing to that place and I see them once again, sleeping in the corner of the room, one beside the other, beneath the brown wool blanket that covered them. I see them, and my heart aches a little, wondering how they are.

The brother soon left, and Ali offered me a bite to eat, but I declined politely. I needed food, but I was not hungry. The tiredness I felt was so encompassing, it left no room for any wants beyond a rich stretch of sleep.

Ali handed me a glass of water, the handcuffs, locked but loosened, and the blindfold. "Rest, and we will see tomorrow," he instructed.

"Thank you," I said. He nodded shyly in acknowledgment, and we both knew that it was neither for the food nor the water.

"If you hear someone coming," he warned, "put on the blindfold and . . . lock the cuffs like before."

"I will," I promised, then went off to my room and closed the door behind me.

Slowly, I tied the blindfold around my head, just above my eyebrows, and placed the handcuffs below my thigh, well within reach should I need them quickly. I leaned back then and began to dream before sleeping. I dreamed of all the people I would see again, of my brothers and sisters. Of hugging my mother and telling her not to cry. I dreamed of the moment I could look around my room, back in the seminary, and see that I was alone and safe, that I did not need to hold myself together any longer. I dreamed of the moment I could collapse without consequence. Wearily I closed my eyes and slept more soundly than I had for what seemed the longest time.

Tea, jam, and bread. The following morning I sat back in the living room, the twins still sleeping in the corner, and quietly ate my breakfast. Ali had left for the day. "I have to go," he had said. "By the afternoon, I will be back, and we will call again and be sure of the situation."

"You couldn't call now?" I had asked.

"When I return," he had told me.

Once my breakfast was finished, I walked quietly back to my room and sat there waiting once again. *God be with me.* I closed my eyes and prayed. Someone is going to come for me. It was the only thing I could be sure of. The liberators or my abductors. Someone was going to come for me.

The night before had opened a wide window, and yet it shrank with every second's passing. Time seemed both slow and fast, and I knew not which to root for. I visualized the second call, imagining the words that would be coming. By the end of the day, I could be home, and all this would be over. I hoped, and worried, for Ali's safety. What would become of him at the end of it? What would he say when I was gone and the others came to collect me? Surely the Americans would take him and his family in. They would not leave them here. It would all play out like a successful liberation. That they had been monitoring a suspected home and luckily they had found me. *God be with me*. Quietly I prayed and waited.

When the front door opened in the midafternoon, I inclined my head to listen. There was no knock. It had to be him, and then the only noise came from the children. He was alone. A half hour later, he was sitting opposite me inside my room, his fingers pushing the buttons of his phone. My nerves jangled as I steeled myself in concentration, though I do not know what it was I was concentrating on. None of it was up to me. Why do people listen so hard when the judge is about to render his verdict? I guess it is so they can keep a grip on their reactions.

"It is Ali," he said, before nodding, gesturing with his hand to tell me that another was being called to speak to him, and he was waiting.

"Yes," he suddenly said, "yes. . . ." I could not take my eyes off him, my shoulders leaning, his every word pulling me closer. "No, he is here, yes, like I say he is here with me . . . yes." Something was wrong, he threw me a quick piercing glance and then looked away immediately. "He is here," he insisted, his free hand gesturing, his words at once sharper in their urgency. "I tell you he is here with me, sitting with me, speak to him."

He handed me the phone, his head shaking in anger and confusion. Could they truly not believe him?

"Why are you doing this?" I asked, barely able to keep from shouting, though I am not overly sure that I wasn't. "Ali is telling you the truth. My name is Saad Sirop Hanna. I have been kidnapped. This is fifteen . . . sixteen days here, and I am a priest. . . ." I could hear my breaths hissing against the phone, but there came no answer. "I am a priest," I repeated, my voice rising in volume. "You know what that means here! You have to come for me. Please come and take me!"

I stopped and waited, a slow second scraped by in silence, and then the man spoke back. "We are very sorry," he said, and for the life of me I could not hear the sorrow in his words. "We do not have orders to come and liberate people from kidnappings. We cannot jeopardize our forces in this way."

The window was closing. My grip was loosening.

"You know what will happen to me. You know what will happen!"

"There are negotiations between the patriarch and the people responsible. You will be liberated." And the line went dead.

The phone hung in my hand. Ali looked at me intently. He wanted to ask, he wanted me to tell him, but he knew already. He knew what it meant, and he did not have any words to add.

That was another of those moments. It contained too many emotions to be condensed into one. Sadness, disappointment, anger, despair. I had been holding onto a rope, its fibers tearing at my hands, and still I had pulled and pulled myself to apparent safety. Then, in an instant, the rope was cut. I had fallen thudding back to ground, and the light was once again very small, very far from me. Ali put the phone back in his pocket, and we both remained silent.

"God willing," said Ali finally. I truly could not know how much time had gone by before he said it. I was dazed with the sound of the monotone line a constant buzz around me. "Maybe, . . ." he began to say, but his voice trailed off to silence.

I imagine it must be similar to what it is like for a lawyer to share a room with a death row inmate when the appeal has returned denied. When they could not find the strength of will to gather up the shards of hope.

"Come," he suddenly said, as he stood and gestured for me to do likewise. "There is something I want to show you." I followed him from the room, past the children and to the door of his home. He stopped a second before cracking it open. "Look," he said, his hand pointing into the far of distance.

An old red car was parked out front. Its wheels and body were caked in light brown dirt, no doubt from frequent trips on the muddy path that stretched behind it. But that was not where his hand was pointing. "Look," he urged, guiding my eyes across the acres of farmland. His was the only home to see; the rest was fields and trees with little else between them.

"Your church," he said. "It is that way!"

I turned to him, then looked again, slowly waking from the daze of disappointment. "There?" I pointed.

"Yes. It is not too far."

All the moves had robbed me of my sense of direction, Suddenly I stared out across the grass and began to calibrate the location. How far exactly? I could not tell, but it was there. Somewhere beyond those fields, somewhere only a handful of miles away was home.

"They have not taken you too far, and God willing, they will soon release you." It was his way of lifting my spirits, and he risked much to do it. I could run. I could strike him then and run. What would he do? If he shot me, would there not be questions for him to answer?

"We need to go back inside," he said.

"You could let me go," I began to say, my voice quickly shrinking.

"I can't," Ali whispered, and I at once felt guilty for asking. I wanted to tell him not to worry. He had done far more for me than I had any right to expect of him. I wanted to tell him that, to tell him that I would not ask again, to say that I was sorry because I had no right to ask. In the end, I simply nodded.

We returned to my room, where he stayed beside me until his brother came, and I heard them talking by the door. "The Americans," Ali was quietly explaining, "they have abandoned him."

The night before I had slept better than any other, and still I felt an utter exhaustion. It was becoming more and more complicated. The Americans, Ali, negotiations, too many people were coming into the equation for a simple outcome. In the evening, Ali returned to my room. He reminded me that they would be coming for me at some point soon, that I needed to be diligent about replacing the handcuffs and the blindfold. "Of course," I told him, and began to place them on in earnest. He stood at the door and looked at me, and when he saw me struggling a little with the cuffs, he stepped inside and knelt to help. "Rest," he said, "God willing, tomorrow will bring good news."

There would be no sleep for me that night, and I cannot recall what thoughts then found me, what prayers if any I incanted. I pulled the blindfold back across my eyes, and the rest was a blur until morning.

It was in the early hours, shortly after the break of dawn, when my door opened abruptly. Ali had received a call. "They are coming for you, very soon, be ready."

"Did they say anything else?" I asked.

"No, but I think they are going to release you. I think this is the end of it."

Release me!

My questions raced off alongside one another, a hundred blind sprinters suddenly set off by the sound of the gun, all clawing for position. How do you know this? But of course he did not know. Then what makes you think it? Why? Why now? What has changed? As his fingers looped and pulled the chain and cuffs around my wrists, checking they were secure, the only question that reached the finish line and emerged from my lips was "How?"

"I think they have contacted your people," he answered, securing the blindfold knot in place. "They must have paid. So . . . once they are sure of the situation, they should release you."

I pondered the thought for a moment. It was a lot to consider all at once so early on a foggy morning. The prickling sense of having to decide on something crawled through me, and I must have looked as though I were about to speak, since Ali stared at me, waiting for a reaction or an answer. But what was there to decide on? It was not for me to rule. They would come and we would see.

"God willing," I finally said.

"God willing," Ali repeated, before he pulled the blindfold down across my eyes and dimmed the day once more to shades of blackness.

Hope is a delicate thing. Just as it can soothe and drive a man to act, it can also slow and delay a man from acting. Quietly I told myself, *The outcome here will not be of my making. They will come and we will see.* Hope was a commodity I could ill afford and I guarded myself against it. *They will simply move you*, I said, without fully believing it, because that is the thing with hope. It's not much given to negative persuasion.

The next part was all routine. The faint hum of a car engine. The front door opening. *Not long, they are here now.* Inaudible words. Ali must have stepped outside to talk to them. Little time passed, and few pleasantries were exchanged. Footsteps. The handle turned. They entered my room. I estimated there were two men, but as ever I could not say this with conviction. They loomed over me.

"Stand," came the order. Two hands gripped my wrist, and I steadied myself as I stood up. Fingers wrapped around the steel, pushing and pulling. I closed my fists and kept my hands steady. When the metal opened, I barely needed to hear the words, "Hands behind your back," and I moved them there. Fists closed again, and the handcuffs were on. The hand guided and I obliged, moving tentatively forward. Down the corridor and onto the soft surface of the mattressed living room. The hour was early, and I imagined when I passed by the twins that they were sleeping, huddled in their corner, unaware of all that was happening and of the world that they had been born to.

The part of me that was not quite in this place wanted to turn to my hosts and thank them for their hospitality. For the drink, the food, the bedding, and the generosity. The door opened, and quietly I stepped out. Specks of gold spread through the shade, and I felt the heat on my face, neck, and shoulders. The ground was rough beneath my shoes, and I stumbled for an instant. I regained my balance but felt the weakness the lack of food had caused. The car was close, just a short walk away. The door opened in front of me, and another man spoke behind me. "Get in." At least two, I reasoned.

My head bowed, I stepped inside, his hand on my back and arm for guidance. "On the floor," he ordered. "Get down." The car was hot, far hotter than the outside. I shimmied from the backseats to the floor, folding in my legs as he shut the door behind me. Another two doors closed. There were two men in the car with me, both sitting upfront. The engine turned on, the car rolled forward, and I heard the sound of another closely following. It was hard to hear, and I tilted my head, grasping for the noise. Suddenly I was sure of it. There were two cars. This was different.

A stale smell filled my nostrils. The car was old, often used, and unwashed. I felt the dirt clinging to my cheeks and turned my mouth away from it. I wanted to reach out and brush it from my face, but I craned my neck around and smeared it across my shoulder. The car sped forward, and I was once again bobbing along in time with the bumps of an unpaved road. Minutes ticked along, with no word from the men upfront. Neither to me nor to each other. I could have asked them if they were exchanging me, but I did not want to allude to the conversations with Ali. Of course, he needn't have said anything for me to think of that. They had told me as much themselves before they took me to him. I could have asked them where we were going, but I didn't for some reason. Just then I felt like waiting.

Were these the same men who had brought me? I played back the basic instructions: *Hands behind your back. On the floor.* The voice was unfamiliar. They might have been the same, but I did not know. Onward we continued—us, and the escort close behind. Still the car shook and dipped as the road crunched beneath it.

"Where now?" one of them asked the other.

"Straight. A little longer."

He didn't know, I thought, and the ember of hope I had tried to extinguish glowed a little brighter. We weren't going to the orchard. *A little longer.* True enough, soon the car began to slow, then moved to the side and stopped.

Desperately, I wished for my eyes to be opened, to be able to see what was coming and prepare myself for it. Were my people waiting here somewhere in the distance? Was this just another change in location? I lay perfectly still and listened closely to any sounds that might help paint the picture. The key turned, the engine stopped, and all fell quiet. Nothing but the rub from the seat in front as the man shuffled and stretched, groaning. Again silence. We were not on the road. There were no other cars, nobody within earshot. And then movement. One of them was doing something. The clicking of the glove box. The rustling of paper. A hand reached into a pocket. The handles were pulled. They stepped outside, and then my door opened. "Sit," he said, reaching in to help me. I jostled back and felt his breath as he leaned close, straining to pull me upward.

I sat up straight. My hands were tied firm behind my back, my one shoulder poking out of the car, the door to my left wide open. The three men gathered there, and I turned to them.

"What are we doing?" I asked.

The one with the directions answered. "We are going to contact your president," he said.

"My president?"

"He will want to talk to you. You understand? He will want to be sure."

I quickly deduced that he was referring to the church, the president being the patriarch of the Chaldean Catholic Church in Babylon, Emanuele Delly.

"Ok," I said, "no problem."

The phone began to beep with every button pressed, every number dialed, and suddenly my mouth felt very dry. I ran my tongue along the inside and swallowed, clearing my throat in preparation.

"Hello. With whom am I speaking?" his tone was deep, deeper than it had been in the car, like an angry man trying to remain calm to solve a problem. "Yes. I will give him to you now."

He placed the open phone to my ear, and I moved my cheek close to it. The reception was poor, and the sound seemed distant, but I could hear it. Someone was on the other line. Someone was listening, and for the first time in seventeen days they would know I was still alive.

"Father Saad?" asked the faint and hopeful voice, and I knew it instantly.

"Yes, Sayidna [Your Excellency]. I am Father Saad."

"Father Saad," the patriarch repeated, no doubt both to me and to whoever was sitting beside him. "Can you please give me the subject and the title of the dissertation you wrote for your master's degree?"

"Yes, Sayidna. . . ." It was an unexpected question, and I hesitated for a second, quickly fanning through the files in my brain for the answer. "The subject was Ibn Rushd . . . the title was 'The Eternity of the World and the Concept of Continuous Creation.'"

I could not tell how well he heard it, or what he had to say to me after. The moment the last word fell from my mouth, the phone was drawn away again.

"So?" my captor asked. "Are you convinced? Let your money be ready."

That was that. They had done what they needed, and we did not linger any longer. With a push I was back on the floor of the car, the door slamming an inch from my head before each man returned to his seat and the car rolled off again.

There was no exchange. After all the words, all the information they had drip fed to me. *Tomorrow you will know. Tomorrow they will come to tell you.* And then they do. And all of it is a lie. There was no exchange, only ransom. How very strange to feel an ounce of disappointment. As though you could expect a grain of truth from the mouths of men who think your murder is their duty. The situation was changing, and I had much to think about, but there was little time. The second part of the drive was far shorter than the first.

Maybe it was when I was pushed down, or else when I was lying flat on the floor, my head bobbing. Either way, the blindfold I wore had inched itself up a little, and as the car was parked and I was ushered out, the sliver of sight my veil allowed was taking in a slightly thicker slice of the picture.

If I could have adjusted it back down, I would have. It was imperative that no one think I had seen them, that I could in any way identify them. Throughout the whole time, I was always very conscious of that. Still, as we walked into the house, I tilted my head ever so slightly, for brief glimpses.

The house was big, a palace of sorts. Of course, abandoned. A little worn and unkempt from lack of use, in the way that buildings get. As we walked onward, another man joined them, one who was here already, and with two men in front and the other guiding me close behind, we passed one room that seemed to house a swimming pool. The tiles below my feet were unmistakable, a faint blue and white in color. Of course, they were covered in dirt and dust, and the pool as far as I could guess was empty, as there was neither the smell of chlorine nor the sound of water.

Someone important had lived here once.

I hate to use that phrase. Money and power do not make one person more important than the other. It is just that they often have more means to alter paths and circumstances.

When we reached a flight of stairs, the man behind warned me of it. He said it in the same terse way they always spoke to me, nothing but the facts. "We are about to climb the stairs," he said, as his hand tightened around my bicep. I placed one exploratory foot and then the other, quickly falling into a rhythm, my eyes looking down, thankful for the widened opening the inched-up veil afforded me. When I had climbed the last step, I stumbled in anticipation of another, but we were at the top, and my guide quickly steadied me. "Forward," he said, and then "stop," when we arrived at our destination.

Once I was led inside a room, my arms were cuffed in the front, and the door was closed behind me. Again I was alone. This had become their way of granting me permission. I would not be told to take off the blindfold, but I would be freed of the impediment of doing so.

Slowly, I lifted it above my head and strained my eyes open. The room was empty. No furniture or bedding or much of anything to speak of. No mattresses. Just white and beige tiles, worn and cracked in many places. I, however, was not looking there. My focus was on the window at the end of the little room.

It had not been opened for some time. The panels were painted white and there was a paint drip that had dried and was suspended near the corner. The metallic handle was buried shut, and I did not think to test it. Perhaps it was not locked, or if it were, and I were able to pry it open, then what? But for allowing in a breath of fresh air, the open window would be little use. It was early afternoon, and the sun was pouring in. I pressed my palms on hot glass and looked down at a portion of an empty yard and a high yellow wall, beyond which very little was visible.

The change was good, I thought, as I sat back down to take stock of what had happened. They had spoken to the patriarch. He knew I was alive. Money was being paid. It was not implausible that they might release me. This might very well be the house where hostages were held before such transactions. Tomorrow, God willing, it might be over.

CHAPTER 9

Kafir

By the evening there was a knock on my door. Two quick raps, not the kind that ask for permission, but those that issue a warning. I had almost drifted off. The room was hot, and I was drenched in sweat and tiredness. Knock, knock. Brief seconds before the door was opened. Hastily I pulled the blindfold down across my eyes, bowing my head so as to avoid inadvertent glances.

The sound of footsteps as two of them entered. "Your hands," said one, and I extended them, clasped tightly, palms upward. He clicked the cuffs in place as the other watched. Tightened the blindfold, told me to stand, then led the way downstairs and out to the courtyard.

Weather is always less extreme indoors. In the lowest temperatures, even if you turn off the heat and the inside is cold, the outside will still be colder. Similarly, when the heat is without mercy, it will not be as hot indoors. When I sat down as instructed, I felt that a part of me was in shade, and I crept toward it. There they left me, and there I would stay for the remainder of daylight. From time to time, I could hear them talking somewhere on the other side of the vast and empty garden. The words were hard to make out, so I could not follow the conversation exactly, but the parts I heard hinted at the rest. It was a familiar conversation that can be heard in every home and tea parlor across Iraq. The most commonly discussed of our issues. The future of the country. They too were concerned, these men, and they wondered what would be next.

Time trickled by, and with the heat, came a greater nuisance. Mosquitos. The same bothersome beasts that would descend on us when we spent the summer nights sleeping on the rooftop. And if that were not enough, there seemed to be a host of other flies and insects, all frantically taking turns to pay me a visit.

Calmness does not sit well with the tired man. His patience does not stretch far, and it does not abide the things of constant annoyance. I was thirsty. Hot. Tired, and burdened with great worry. The incessant buzzing close to my ears, the pinches on my arms and face and neck, the itchy skin, and the hands restricted from getting to it, were a constant drip drop on my temperament. At first I shook my head when the buzzing sound grew closer, louder. I jerked my arms when I felt something crawling on them, but after a while, I did it less. Resistance was futile.

Soon the crickets began to chirp, and the shadow beneath my veil turned blue and darker. "Take it," said a voice, and I heard the crunch of a plastic bottle, the noise of the drink swirling inside it. "Here," he urged, tapping the base against my knuckles, before I blindly grabbed it from his hand and chugged back a mouthful in one quick motion.

None of them had come to me until then, and, when the man seemed to be lingering, I decided it was a fair chance to start a conversation.

"The river?" I asked.

"Huh?"

"The sound," I said pointing a finger to my right, while holding firm to the bottle he had given me. "Is that the sound of water?"

"Yes," he grunted, "that is the river."

I nodded, wondering if I should press on with another question, perhaps about where I was headed. Would he even know? But before I asked, it was he who broke the silence.

"We used to swim in there," he said, "when we were younger."

"Yes?"

"Yes, but the water is no good anymore. Not nice like before."

"Why is that?"

"Before, it was natural," he said. "It is dirty now. Too many bodies, too much blood."

Say what you will about this man, but he sure knew how to kill a budding conversation. There were no more questions from my side. He walked back to the others, and I was thankful for the solitude.

As the night wore on, it seemed that I was not the only one being bothered by the onslaught of insects, and my companions had a curious method for dealing with the problem. It began with a whiff of a foul smell, which grew stronger. "Yes, yes, more," one would say, as the others brought and poured.

Manure. Mounds and mounds of it. And more. A miniature hill quickly growing.

The senses have a way of bookmarking our memories. The more uncommon the touch, the scent, or the sound, the greater the attachment to it remains. Still sharp. Unused and unblunted. If not through the strong sensory impression, then through the uniqueness of the memory itself, of its importance. That song that played in the backdrop of a singular moment. The smell of a dish your mother cooks, the one that fills the house and finds you stepping in from the cold. These are the trapdoors of time, and there are some you don't ever want to fall back through.

The smell of the manure was bad enough, but soon came the canisters. The ping of hollow metal flexing and shaking. Of liquid spilling out. The noxious waft of petrol. They poured it on the manure, scratched a match or two, and lit the pile on fire. Now *that* was a smell. Too thick for any other to claw its way through it. With the occasional pop, the fire burned on, and I imagined the mounds of waste sizzling inside of it. With every breath, I swallowed that foulness. My stomach seized, and I clasped my arms close to my chest to stop from retching, pulling quick sips from my water bottle, and quickly covering the lid with my hands for fear that it too would start to carry the taste of my surroundings.

As the night wore on, and the flames fell silent, it became apparent that the outdoors was where we would be sleeping.

It was then that a man approached me, delivering a small blanket and some advice.

"The bugs will eat you in the night," he said, as I pulled the thin wool blanket tight across my arms. "Move to the left and down, and they will let you be." To the left and toward the smell and piled-up sludge of melted shit. I cannot remember thanking him for that piece of wisdom, but the bugs were mauling me and in his words there was indeed a useful instruction.

What was a yard or two anyhow?

I shuffled closer and closer, and only drew away when I felt the first squish of wet paste beneath my probing fingers. There I lay. Escaping the bugs by huddling beneath the gasses emanating from the pile of manure beside me.

I longed so very much to sleep, to close my eyes and be transported from this intrusive reality. However, it would be a restless night. Down on the ground, I lay and thought of all of it. Struck by wave after wave of grainy facts and untold complications. Of the muddy tracks my days had taken, of the things we do, the plans we make, and the wants we fall prey to. I thought of the world in total, of all of us, of how we cease to simply be people to one another, becoming more but so very much less. The night was hot, but I felt my body shivering inside of it. "The water is no good anymore," the man had said. "It's dirty now. Too many bodies, too much blood." He was right, and I thought of that, and of the sights that had greeted me three years before, when I first returned.

The year was 2003, and barely a month had passed since we had all seen the scene on television, of the large iron statue of Saddam Hussein breaking at the ankles and slowly falling. Pulled down by ropes across the neck and torso, and dragged through the dirt while some crowds cheered and some children chased behind it.

The summons was a surprise. I, along with some of my class-mates, had just completed my master's degree and was preparing to continue my studies. My ambition was to earn the doctorate in philosophy. That had been the plan for some time, and all the work I had put in was geared toward it. Plans do often change, however, and at the Chaldean Synod, which is the official meeting of the patriarch and the Chaldean bishops, it was decided that all the priests studying abroad would be asked to return. Our country was facing a most turbulent time, and no man could be spared from assisting. In a telephone call, the bishop told us that. He said that the patriarch wished for us to make a decision: to remain in Rome, and see our studies through to the end, or to return to Iraq in this most difficult time and begin our mission of assisting the people. Naturally, all four of us returned.

There are some coincidences in life that are outside the realm of the probable. The four of us had caught a flight to Jordan, and on the sixth of October 2003, we booked a car and crossed the border onto Iraqi soil. I never struggle to remember that day, not only because of what I felt and saw but because it would be three years to the day that I would leave again, a man much changed.

It is the same with most things, be they places or people; some years are more shaping than others. I had not been back to my country since 1998, and in those five years, much had changed. All around, you could not but see traces of it. To me, it seemed very different.

As we passed over the border, and the vast barren landscape of the long road that followed it, and onto the streets of the Baghdad we all once knew, we stared in thoughtful silence through the windows of our car. Tourists in our own country. The many years of embargo had previously placed a tired tint on the roads and buildings that bordered them. That much we remembered. The place we had left was not vibrant with polished color. Even then, the buildings had been worn and were crying for repair. Yet this was different. It was not the long-suffering patient, who had amassed more wrinkles than his age warranted, but the one who had just recently fallen, could barely stand, and was staggering on his feet.

The aftermath of the many airstrikes had left marks all around us: in the rubble along the streets; in the holes gaping from the buildings, framed by protruding bars of metal, like open mouths with broken teeth; in the people who swarmed about looking both purposeful and lost; in the lines and lines of barbed-wire fences glistening in the sun; and in the tanks and Humvees and the many foreign soldiers who accompanied them.

It was as though a giant had fallen. The earth below him rumbled. And a cloud of dust had risen to cover him.

However, along with the sadness I felt from the sights I saw, there too remained the promise of much beauty. I carried many things besides the suitcase filled with my old shirts and new priest's clothing. I carried the knowledge I had gained, the product of years of study—theological and philosophical science, new languages, and a deeper understanding. The tools I would use to benefit my people. Above all that, what I brought back with me on that journey was the hope for a new beginning. It is easy for a person to become mired in pessimism, and the world can very ably assist in sustaining such a feeling. And any man can look back on the death and destruction of that war and claim to have foretold the unsettled, blood-filled years that would follow. I, however, though absolutely not ignorant of the difficulties, was optimistic for the future. A monumental change had befallen Iraq and its people, but the values professed by the conquerors or liberators, however one may view them, were nonetheless worthy of our aspiration. Democracy, freedom, and the sacred protection of human dignity. I believed that instead of weeping for what we had lost, we must endeavor to seize this chance and build anew. And I had returned to find myself a useful place in those efforts.

Near enough three years later, I reflected on that time as I was handcuffed and blindfolded, lying beside a pile of manure, not knowing if I would live to see the following morning, listening to the sounds of my sleeping guards, on the seventeenth day of my captivity. There I saw how wrong I had been about so much. The people who had come were ill prepared to carry out the changes they had promised us. Perhaps they were also too optimistic about the ease of the transition, though it may be doing them an underserved kindness to presume so. The reality had been far harsher and far more complex than I could have reasoned. I had not returned at the end of the war but merely at a new beginning.

"Wake up! Wake up!" It may have been his words or else the kick of his boot that woke me. Either way it did not matter as both were stuck firmly on repeat.

"Wake up!" he said in a shouted whisper, the kind where the person needs to scream but cannot for fear of elevating the very danger he is screaming about. My cuffed hands were bent beneath my head as a makeshift pillow, and the point of his boot struck me in the stomach.

"I am awake! I am awake!" I said in urgent protest, my eyes blinking open to the lighter darkness beneath my veil. Confusion is not uncommon when you are stirred suddenly from a state of deep sleep. Normally it would be a matter of seconds, two or three, as the facts were sifted through the sieve of reality, and the brain quickly separated the dream from the true present. It is how we calm ourselves after a nightmare, except in my case, when the facts were finally settled, the nightmare was what remained.

"Stand," he ordered, before quickly switching his attention to the others. "Stand him up." Hands on me from either side, fumbling for a grip. I moved up, pushing out my elbows, making it easier for the men to assist me.

"Bring him," he ordered.

"Where?" another asked, and as I felt the three of them pause for an answer or a plan, I became awake once more to my surroundings. And as I did, I heard the noise that seemed to be the source of their alarm.

High up, somewhere in the skies above us, far away and loud enough to be too close, I heard the unmistakable drill and gust of a helicopter flying overhead.

"To the car," came the slightly unsure instruction, yet it was certain enough for action, and to the car we went, the two men taking hurried steps while I peddled between them. Trying hard to arch my toes and keep apace, so as to stop my shoes from slipping off, I heard the key turn inside the lock with some haste and the boot pop open.

"Put him in," one said. A quite unnecessary instruction, as why else would they have rushed me there to begin with? They pushed and I maneuvered as best I could in an effort to ease this unavoidable transition, until I was safely tucked inside and the box came to a thudding close.

I cannot say with full certainty, but I believe it must have been early in the morning, no later than six or seven. There I remained for quite some time with little change, or at least for a lengthy time, when considering I had been awoken with a kick and then another, rushed unseeing to the car, bundled inside the boot that was swiftly slammed above me. Perhaps it was an hour or an hour and a half. Either way, the men seemed to leave, and there was little for me to hear beyond the sound of my own breathing. The car was still, and I reasoned that they had placed me there just to remove me from view, and not for the purpose of transferring me.

Could that helicopter have actually been searching for me? Perhaps the call to the patriarch had alerted those seeking me to something, of whom they were dealing with and where I could plausibly be taken. I wondered then if I actually wanted them to find me, of what would happen if they did. A rescue attempt. The first thing my captors would do in such a circumstance would probably be to kill me. What would that take? One second, one turn, one shot, and then they could focus only on escaping. I thought that my chances would not play so well in that scenario, but there was little use in considering it. Ali had told the Americans exactly where I was, and where I would be for the remainder of that night, ready and unguarded, and still they did not wish to come for me. What would make them want to do so now?

After some time passed, I was not taken back into the house or to the courtyard. Instead the car doors opened and closed, and we were once more on our way to a familiar destination.

Another drive. The air was becoming ever thinner in my compartment. In times like these, I would close my eyes and regulate my breathing, so that my breaths were not too deep and not too frequent. A calming meditation. Still we rumbled onward, and still I breathed and still I hoped. I hoped for the end of it, for an exchange, and for release. Or failing that, then at least a shorter drive to the next destination. The latter of my hopes would be fulfilled.

Soon enough, the car slowed, the wheels wheezing on the turn, maneuvering to park. The engine stopped, doors opened, air gusted in as the boot was lifted up and then down again, and my feet found the ground. A hand on my shoulder, I walked a few yards forward to the next place, no doubt another room where I would be kept, when suddenly I heard a familiar voice calling.

"What, they haven't set you loose?" he asked. The Chair Man, the one who first spoke to me of prisoner exchanges. The hand on my shoulder tightened, and we stopped. He was the one, I thought. I had known from the first time I heard him. He was the leader of this group.

"You should know," I said, keeping my head and blind gaze forward, though the direction his voice was coming from placed him at my right. "You should know why you have not let me go. Did you not receive your money? Why are *you* not releasing me?" My voice was tired, but I felt a strength in speaking, as though I had been unsure of having the words until I uttered them.

"Yes, yes, soon," he said. "God willing, in two days." There he left it, and I did not ask him for any details. "Take him inside," he ordered the others, and I was hurriedly led a short distance, down a short corridor and back into a little room.

My hands were cuffed in the front, and when the door closed, I lifted the blindfold to take a quick look at my surroundings. From the presence of the Chair Man, I suspected I was back near the orchard, but the room was different from the last that had housed me. No chairs or furnishings. No carpet on the floor and no paint on the walls. The place seemed incomplete, or else it was never meant to have a man live in it. From dark gray cement, bare bricks bulged in rows, rough and not quite even. It looked cold, but it wasn't. A place to store produce before moving. My room for at least the night.

Sleep as ever came in fits and starts, but I felt strong. I would close my eyes and drift into prayer. God was with me, and I knew it. It was the purpose of all of this that still eluded me, and I prayed for clarity, for the strength not to surrender for the sake of the shallowness of ease and comfort. When the morning came, my situation among these people began to worsen.

It was seven or eight. Hard to tell as the room held no windows. No knock before my door swung open. I had moved to the corner, my back against one wall and my shoulder on the other. My legs stretched out, hands cuffed to the front and the blindfold firmly on. Two men entered, and immediately, I heard a difference in their strides. Heavy, purposeful, and fast. In a second, they were close, hovering above me.

"Stand up, sheep!" screamed one. "Stand up!"

Wide awake before they had entered, I quickly placed my palms on the wall to my left and moved to stand, but as I did a forceful kick across my thighs sent me tumbling backward.

"Today," pronounced one, "you will become a Muslim!"

"I will not," I shouted.

"You will not?" the man screamed back, our voices echoing in the little room we occupied.

"I cannot."

"Why?" he asked. Then it came, the first of them, catching me blind, half on the knuckles of my right hand and across my cheek and ear. Back I fell, my head buzzing from the impact, and then came another and another and another. The wooden sticks whipping through the air as they stuck me. And that same question, from one, from the other, and from both. "You will not become a Muslim?"

I wasn't even answering anymore. "What is this?" I asked. "Why are you hitting me? You are not afraid of God?"

"Kafir," would be their reply as they continued. Slumped low, hands cuffed, and blindfold on, I felt the blows, but knew not from where and when they would come. My hands gripped one another tight above my head, bracing for each impact, my body curling into a ball in the corner as they continued to ask and beat me. Strike after strike, and with each, the pain like an electric shock pulsed through me. The sticks were stiff, and I remember hoping that at some point they would break on impact.

When another landed squarely on my back, I arched downward, afraid that they would crack the bone and cause me lasting damage.

Then, suddenly, the frequency of the blows slowed. "Kafir," the one said, as he delivered the final vicious strike before the two of them walked out, closing the door behind them.

Kafir. It is a powerful word. "Kafir" means unbeliever or infidel. A word that is often not fully comprehended and understood. How can you wish for untold horror and destruction? Kafir. How can you maim and hate and butcher? Kafir. How can you destroy the lives of so many innocent people? Kafir. All this you can do when your victims are not innocent. I was not innocent to them. I was a kafir. Guilty of sin and faithlessness. There are some Wahhabi Muslims who believe that a Christian does not fall within the definition of kafir, and there are those who would allow a Christian a special reprieve of taxation, yet for those who deem any non-Muslim to be kafir, there are few dispensations beyond conversion. It is a stifling realm devoid of the air that is necessary for reason to breath. A place of unequivocals. I am a sinner. They are not.

I was not lying down but was instead half slumped near the ground, a heaped up mound of a man. Afraid to move because of the pain. My thighs, hips, and back had taken most of the blows, with my back hurt the most. The slightest motion sent a twinge that robbed me of breath, as though my whole body had seized to prevent me from further movement, and so I stayed still. There I remained. My frame as still as could be, while my fingers gently felt about for clues to the true extent of the damage. I edged the blindfold up and cranked my head to see, but it was hard to tell. Blindfold back to its original place, I sat and slowly calmed myself. It was not just the pain but what it meant for me.

"No one will harm you here," the Chair Man had said on the third day of my abduction, and up until then, it had been true. Now things had taken a turn for the worse. I did not know what had changed, but I could not shake the thought that this was the beginning of the end for me. Even though the possibility of rescue had been remote before, suddenly it had grown slimmer.

It was not until the afternoon that the door opened once again, and my immediate instinct was to cower—to shuffle back, to somehow protect myself—but I managed to resist it. With my legs crossed, I placed my hands in my lap and waited for whatever was coming.

In the few times I had spoken to him, he never was alone. With two others, the Chair Man entered. Though I had begun to differentiate between the people through minor sounds and little tell-tale giveaways, still I could not know for sure until they spoke.

"You are an educated man," he said, his thick voice sounding two or so meters ahead of me.

"I have studied," I answered, "for a long time."

"Yes, well there is a chance for you. A way with which *you* can save yourself."

He paused. I guess waiting for me to ponder the possibilities and to ask him how, but I didn't. I knew full well what he meant. It was that same question the two had asked me in the morning. I knew the question and the answer to it.

"If you became a Muslim, you could build a life here. You could rescue yourself and live."

"I cannot," I said, "at the very least not under these conditions."

"An educated man could be useful here. You could be of use educating the young ones. You could be a teacher."

"I *am* a teacher."

"And you will be one once again."

"The decision you speak of, it cannot be made in the circumstances I am in," I said, holding up my handcuffed hands. "Release me. Allow me to leave and I . . . will think on it clearly."

"Release you and you will think on it," he repeated with a thin hint of skepticism in his voice. That was the thing with this man, he was nearly impossible to gauge. The words simply rolled out of him, one by one, as though they were being efficiently selected and passed down by the arm of a machine, each knowing its place, and awaiting its turn. It was hard to tell too much as you could never feel the color.

"I will," I said forcefully. "That I can promise you, but more than that I really cannot offer."

There were no more words between us then, and he left the room before I could talk of the injuries his men had inflicted upon me. The truth was I did not want to. I knew he knew, and there was a defiance in not giving in to useless complaining, in not elevating his authority, in not asking him to reprimand the others. To tell them to cease from such actions. It was he who had assured me, and it was his word that was broken. To me his word was no longer to be trusted, no longer of any use. What reason would I then have to ask for it?

An hour or so later, the two men returned alone to take me. The usual procedure. Stand. Walk. Ushered to the car, and to the backseat carpet. From there, I would be returned to the orchard, and back to Abu Hamid.

CHAPTER 10

The Sniper, the Butcher, and the Dogs

"You!" I heard the voice somewhere outside of my thinking. The afternoon was waning on, and its yellow tint had become the blue and black of early evening. The pain of the morning's visit had given way to a quiet aching. Sitting on the grassy ground of the orchard, I was feeling both tired and lazy.

"You," the man said, his voice ringing closer. "What would you do if the Americans come?"

What would I do? It was not so simple a question, and I could sense him waiting for the answer. It is not always good to say the first thing that pops into your mind, not only because you want to be mindful, but because it may not be the truth. What would I do? I guess I would wait to see what was happening. How close they were. How great the danger. What my viable options might be. I did not say any of that. Instead I shrugged my shoulders.

"If the Americans raid this place and you run, . . ." he began to warn, his words becoming more resolved, letting me know how serious he was about the consequences, even though I never doubted him, "or shout, or move, or get up and make a noise, I will shoot you where you stand. The first thing I will do is put a bullet in your head."

He prodded my temple with his finger, and I could feel his excitement growing at the thought of it as the machine gun rattled in his hands.

"Look," I calmly said in an appeal for reason, "I can't see, but if it happens, you put your hand in mine and I will run with you. Just take my hand, and we can run. Don't you have to steer me?"

"Yes," he said, "fine," as though he were approving my proposal. After that he returned to his companion, and I went back to sitting there.

Nineteen days in captivity, and but for Abu Hamid and the Chair Man, I could not distinguish my abductors from one another. Much like the unheard tick tock of the hours, the voices and the insults of these unseen men smudged into a single blot.

"What if the Americans come?" this one had asked. They must have been afraid of it. Of such raids. Of the Americans finding them. That must be the constant danger of their daily lives, and it explained the earlier panic at the sound of a helicopter. How many stories do they have? I wondered, of someone they used to know. A friend? A cousin? A father? A son? A sister? A brother? How many times did they have to knock on a door and break the news? And how often were they the ones left standing on the opposite side, picking up the pieces? Such things can never be imagined. When seeing it befall another, people cannot but remember the losses they themselves have faced, and yet they know that none are perfectly alike. Love was never meant to be easy. Even for a man such as myself, one who wholeheartedly believes in the eternity of the spirit, it still offers no immunity from the gnawing sting of loss. It takes courage to open one's self to this inevitable heartache, yet that is what a life of love demands of us, and it is what we must do, for that truly is the only kind of life worth living.

That night we stayed alone, three of us, outside in the orchard, beneath what I imagined to be a black and starry sky.

While they slept, I bowed my head and turned to God. A gesture I had for years performed, at times quite unthinkingly, throughout the day, and more so whenever I was at my late night prayer, was then impeded twice over.

Gold, neither cheap nor overly expensive, with a thin figure of Christ, head slightly bowed to the side, intricately sculpted—the cross I had worn every day for the past two years was a gift from my mother. For most of my life I had worn one, and yet this one was different. My father had passed, and she traveled, along with others from our family, the long journey to Rome, so she could be present on the day of my ordination. The day on which I would officially become a priest. The cross was her gift to me on that occasion. Accepting the cross from her hands, I fastened the chain behind my neck, and not a single day had passed from then on without it being with me.

Not until some two years later, on the fifteenth of August, the day of my abduction. When, after visiting the church in the morning to aid and oversee the early preparations, I returned to the seminary for an afternoon nap, knowing, and nowhere near knowing, that I would have a busy day ahead me, I removed the cross and placed it in the top drawer of the bedside cabinet. And when I woke, an hour later, so concerned was I with remembering the sermon I had written, that for the first time since I had had it, I forgot the cross and left without it.

Quite unthinkingly throughout the day, and more so in my late night prayers, I would reach to my chest to touch it. Whether it was the one my mother had given me, or any other I had worn during my life, the feel of it inside my hands was a source of strength and purpose.

In my nineteenth night away from home, by habit I moved my hands to touch the cross, and felt them cuffed behind me. Even if it had been there, I could not have reached to touch it.

It can be tempting to see great meaning in such things, to wonder if I had been abducted because I lacked the protection this gift, a symbol of God, had afforded me, and yet it is not so. The cross is a symbol of the infinite love of God, a love so vast that he would send his only son as a sacrifice for our salvation. It hangs around the necks of millions of men and women around the world, not as a plea to God for help when needed, but as a pledge to offer help to those who need it. That is the way of Christ, and I did not need the cross against my chest to feel it.

My Lord, it seems that the end for me here is nearing, and if it is, then I am ready. If this is your purpose for me, then I accept it, and I am ready.

"For it has been granted to you on behalf of Christ, not only to believe in him, but also to suffer for him"

I had not planned for the circumstances in which I found myself. I had neither wished for it nor even given much thought to its occurring. However, this life was of my choosing. I had dedicated myself to following the example of Christ, and, in the righteousness of my suffering, to endure through no act of hatred but solely through the openness of a love unyielding and unconquered; in that, I felt a closeness to him and to the purpose of my being, and it gifted me with a greater strength and joy than I had ever known was possible. I was determined that they would not break me. That I would not give up who I was for the sake of longevity. *It will get worse from here*, I reasoned. Though a hot rush of fear coursed through me at the prospect, I vowed both to God and to myself that no matter what was coming, I would not perish to survive.

The following morning, the strikes came again with little warning.

Waking at this point meant mainly that I stopped attempting to sleep. At some time around the break of dawn, after I heard my companions rise, move about, and gather up the nighttime bedding, they unbound my legs and escorted me a short distance to a tree in the orchard. There, against the bark, they left me while they went about their morning prayers. Twenty days with little food and little drink had reduced me to feeling as though I lived underwater, where every movement was slow and labored, pushing against an invisible force, sapping me of energy.

My arms were growing stiff from being folded behind me, and I stretched them gently to shake away the numbness, careful not to rush, as though the bruises on my back and shoulders were landmines on which I had to tread ever so lightly, so I could pause and withdraw when the pain screamed out their presence.

There were no words this time when they returned to me, an hour or two later, no invitations to conversion or questions about why I resisted. This was more for punishment, or amusement. The first blow came from the side, rattling the bone of my elbow, and I barely had time to move, to duck, to brace myself for what I knew would follow, when another landed squarely on my back and the downpour started. Hit after hit, as the two men swung the sticks with full ferocity. Spitting the word *kafir* in between their grunts of exertion. "Kafir," they would shout, and the stick would strike down harder, as though they drew power from invoking reason for the abuse. "Kafir" and the stick would whistle in the instant before impact, whipping at the bruises I had formerly moved so gently to avoid, exploding the landmines of pain along my back as I struggled to draw a gulp of breath, pulling at shallow air before the next hit hiccupped it from out of my lungs to leave me drowning where I knelt. With my hands still cuffed behind my back I could not raise them to my head, I could not protect myself in any way from what was happening. All I had were words, and yet I did not utter them. I did not scream for them to stop, I did not ask them once again if they feared the very God they aimed to serve. I would not give them the reward of my protestations. It was then when another screamed for me.

"Why are you doing this?" he shouted. Abu Hamid had come to take his shift that morning, and my being beaten was the sight that greeted his arrival. "Why are you hitting him?" he asked as he hurried closer.

"Silence!" the man who leaned above me ordered as he swung the stick back down again. "You have no business in this."

I knew it then for sure, the truth in what Abu Hamid had once told me. He had no power in any of it. Just a watchman with few alternatives, who did as he was told. Silently he stood and watched. Silently he watched as they stuck me once again, a final flurry, just to prove the point that they could, and then it stopped. My eyes clenched shut beneath the veil in prayer. *God give me strength. Give me strength my Lord,* I pleaded without speaking aloud. The two men walked away, and I remained as still as could be, afraid again that, with the meagerest movement, the bells of pain would begin ringing.

When the two men left, and Abu Hamid and I remained alone an hour or so later, he came to me. I winced as the key scratched about the lock behind my back before it clicked the cuffs open. Slowly, he moved my arms forward, the metal ring dangling from my right wrist. "Take some water," he said, pushing the cup into my hands, and I drank from it. It was hot but soothing.

"Are you ok?" he asked, and I could hear the genuineness of his concern.

"Why are you doing this? You have received your money. Why would you not release me?"

"Truthfully, I do not know," he protested, taking the cup back from my hands. "I have no connection to this."

"Of course you do."

"I do not know why they are doing it. I truly think they want to release you."

"They would have done it already. No. I am going to die here. I know that now. You people are going to kill me."

"No, no, don't say that. God willing, your family will pay and then they will release you. Soon, God willing."

"My family?" I asked.

"Yes, they must be waiting for that payment. Then I honestly believe they will release you."

More payments. More complications. It seemed though there were reasons to keep me alive, there were few reasons to set me free. Once again, the thin odds of survival were becoming ever thinner.

With Abu Hamid's help, I walked back to the spot where I had slept the night before. There, he cuffed my hands again, and there we remained, just the two of us, until the following morning.

Half asleep, I did not hear them come until they started talking, and the conversation was not one you would wish to listen to.

Five, at a guess. One of the problems with deciphering voices through sound is that once the number becomes greater than three, determining how many are there becomes guesswork, especially when the tones are unfamiliar. They were not the same men who had been with me those nights before. Not the same men who doled out the beatings, and if there was a relief in that, then I did not have the time to feel it.

"Why are we keeping him?" the one asked. "Let's finish it now!"

Standing not far away, they spoke while paying little mind to what I heard.

"Nobody has told us otherwise," replied another. "Should we not wait until they say?"

"What's the use in it?"

"Well it is not like this. If they say it, we do what's needed, but they haven't, and someone is coming to take him today. To move him somewhere else."

"Finish him and be done with it," the man said in exasperation, as though my being alive were a nuisance.

I could not but marvel at how easy it seemed to them. For the entirety of my adulthood, I have sought to preach love to those who would listen and those who would not. I spoke of tolerance in the face of judgment, of seeing the many things that unite us rather than those that divide us, of recognizing that no matter how vast our differences may seem, we will always be one people. And yet there I sat, early in the morning, shackled and beaten, listening as my life teetered on the outcome of a conversation.

Like an army of ants crawling beneath my skin, anger began to infest me. A tremor in the foundation of a long-held belief, a crack in faith so deep that I instantly knew it would be lasting. The years might fade it, but the scar would remain. People often question whether a man may abandon his faith in God when he is faced with a continuous torrent of wickedness. My faith in God was as strong as it had ever been. I was angry at the evil I had come to witness. I was angry at how these men in their hatred had failed my family, how they had failed my church, my people, and our country. The Iraqis I had heard of in my parents' stories, and the Iraqis I had known throughout my years, were filled with goodness, with love, and with compassion. Never had I dreamed before that they would be capable of such atrocities. It seemed clear then that the years of war had like a sickness infected the very core of our being. My faith in God was as strong as it had ever been. It was my faith in humanity that wavered.

That afternoon, just as the man had said, a car pulled up to move me. This time to a different place altogether.

Before the drive, they exchanged their hellos and placed me in my usual space in the car boot. If any good had come of the conversation I had overheard, then it was that no order had yet been given for my execution. A definite silver lining, all things considered. Therefore, I was not overly nervous about this latest movement, but was only anxious that it be done in as smooth a manner as possible. The confinement of these trips, though always arduous owing to the heat and lack of oxygen, was now causing an added discomfort from the cuts and bruises that riddled my back and shoulders. Still I continued to take steady, even breaths, ably calming myself, especially when the bumps in the road sent pulses of pain throughout my body. It would be less than an hour before we slowed and stopped at our destination.

Without uttering any words or instruction, my two new companions opened the boot and brought me to what I presume was the home of one of them. But we never went inside the house itself. Instead, we walked to the side, to a narrow pass, where the one man placed both hands on my shoulders to steer me. I could still feel the wall occasionally rubbing on my elbows as we made our way to the rear of his home, and to the garden.

There was little by way of talk or a greeting when we entered, and yet I felt as though others were there already, and not just one or two but more. What brought about that feeling I cannot say for sure. Perhaps I had heard their sounds earlier, before they had grown quiet with my arrival. Whatever the reason, soon they would all be comfortable enough to talk, and the fact of their presence would be readily apparent.

"Sit," the one told me, as I heard the other walking off into the house, the door closing behind him. "Like this," my guardian clarified, with a firm hand pulling at shoulder, turning me around where I crouched, until I was nestled in some unknown corner.

"Al Salaam Alaikum" (peace be upon you), I heard him say in greeting. "Wa Aliakum Salaam" (and upon you peace), came the customary reply from a few others. It was not an exceptionally large garden, though it was hard for me to estimate the size with any precision. I was sitting at the end closest to the house, and they at the other.

It was early evening, and I could hear the sound of children playing on the other side of the wall beside me, of a mother speaking to them, of clothes flapping in the wind, no doubt to be hung on the washing line. It was a village. A small, rural one. The home was not isolated. There were others to either side, and cars could be heard from time to time somewhere in the distance. Men returning home, perhaps, at the end of a day of work. Someone utterly unfamiliar with the areas in which I had found myself, then, might think shouting out, alerting people of my presence, was a good idea. I, however, was not tempted by such a thought, aware that doing so would undoubtedly be more likely to place me in extreme danger than to benefit me.

"Make some food for us," the man walked over to the house and shouted to his wife. The smell of seared onions, and then tomato sauce soon began to waft from inside, teasing at my hunger. I would get my share, but I did not want it, not a lot anyhow, just a little, just enough so that I could keep on going. She would not come out, of course, not while there was company present. Instead he went inside and fetched the food out for his companions, myself included.

The plate rattled with the clink of a spoon as he placed it on the ground in front of me, the cup beside it. "Eat," he said, after unlocking my handcuffs, by which he meant for me to lift the blindfold from my eyes a little. I waited a few seconds before doing so, my head bowed as it always was in the presence of others, so that I would not see more than I wished to. There was a brick wall at my right shoulder, and I turned to gently lean my back against it, pulling the plate up to my folded legs. A chunk of meat lay in the middle, surrounded by chopped green peppers, onions, and tomato sauce. Quite appetizing under normal circumstances. I drank a swallow of water and felt it slide roughly down the dryness of my throat. A second passed, and then I drank another.

The others, somewhere at the end of the garden to my right, were thanking the host as they crowded around the food he was serving them. They had not been speaking much, and when they did, I was not straining to listen. I had grown tired of that, of trying to piece together clues from men who might not be able to tell me much, even if they decided to speak frankly. I was happier siting alone in quiet thought, until they called to me.

The spoon was halfway to my mouth when I heard it. "You know who gave that food to you?" the voice called out. I shook my head. "Huh? You know who gave that food to you?" he asked again.

"No," I said, without turning, my eyes directed squarely at the plate in front of me.

"That is The Butcher," he proudly announced. "How many?" he asked of his friend, who I guess in modesty refrained from answering. "Twenty eight, yes?" the man pressed on. "Twenty eight men, all by his sword. The Butcher!" He laughed at that, and I drank another sip of water, my mouth still very dry.

A while later, once the food had been taken away and my hands had been cuffed once again, this time in front, a few others arrived. A few men and two dogs that barked incessantly. I did not know it then, but soon enough, I would meet the dogs close up.

The evening had ticked on, and all that was left was the black of nighttime. It is hard to describe such nights, when the injuries and fatigue take hold of you and create a different kind of consciousness. Absolutely I was aware of all of my surroundings. It was just that the pathways of thought would wind so far away from physical reality that I would find that my body had stayed perfectly still for longer than an hour before I would turn or twitch and notice it. And when I did it was as though the lights flickered on and everything around me became louder for a second while I readjusted.

"From a kilometer!" they were the words I heard when it happened to me that time, and then that laugh again.

"Even flying?"

"In the air from a kilometer I downed him. Believe me."

They were swapping stories, boasting of deeds, making small talk and, as ever, discussing politics. It was then that he turned to me again with a question.

"You," he called. "What do you think?"

"Of what?" I wearily answered.

"Of now, of course, of this Iraq. Is it better now, or under Saddam?"

I had not spoken for a while, and I did not wish to shout back to him, but I had to reply, and I well knew the answer that he wanted.

"Better under Saddam," I said. It was not improbable that some of these men had had an affiliation with the old regime, and it was extremely likely that they opposed whoever was in power now. However, that was not why I said it. I did not say it with an aim to please.

"Why better with Saddam?" he asked, and the others all fell silent, waiting.

"Because . . ." I began, pausing to clear my throat, "if Saddam were still present, you would not be able to come to the church and take me."

Without quite saying yes, he grumbled in thought, and none of them denied it.

Most of the men soon left, and I and the two remaining slept much as I had the past few nights beneath the sky outside. Twenty-one nights had passed with me in captivity, and on the twenty-second morning, I was awoken at the break of dawn.

"Get up! Get up!" they said, kicking me from out of the fragile sleep I had finally stumbled into.

It was perhaps five or six in the morning. It could not have been a great deal later. The light was pale beneath the veil, barely out of full darkness. Just a drop or two of white in a sea of black. I moved up to rest on my elbows, eager to show them that I was awake, and the kicking stopped. What do you do when something wakes you an hour earlier than the alarm you had set? How do you feel? Going back to sleep was not an option. Nor was simply lying there a while, waiting for the senses to slowly find their rhythm. My body ached, my mouth was dry, and my head was foggy. As I slowly shuffled to my knees, a sudden bout of dizziness came over me. Impatiently, the man reached over and jerked me upward. There was no time to dawdle, and so I stood.

Into the house and up the stairs we went. Everything was so quiet that the sound of each step we took echoed, and I wondered why this early movement? Perhaps a precaution.

A door opened, and they walked me the length of a small room. "Sit," they ordered before leaving.

Turning up the blindfold a little, I pried my eyes open and looked about this new enclosure. There was not much to see, a small bare rectangular room, with the door on one end and me on the other. This must be where I was to stay for the next part of the day. At least I might be able to sleep for an hour, I thought. I was careful not to waste the rare opportunities to rest, when I knew that I could quickly drift to sleep.

It felt like a blink. No sooner had my eyes closed, then they opened once again at the sound of the door. I did not know for sure then, but in hindsight, it could not have been much longer than ten or so minutes before the two men returned to me.

"Sit up!" the one man shouted, far louder than necessary. It was the noise at first. The hurried steps, the sniffs, and the panting. Mobile, on the move, busy. Then the smell, not unpleasant, quite familiar, a sweaty combination of stale earth and fresh grass. With my back against the wall, I sat as still as could be, my muscles taut in anticipation, as the two men and the two dogs moved toward me.

I never really saw them, but close your eyes and imagine the noise. The bark, at first one, rumbling from out of a growl, and then two close together. You hear it, and you see a little. The dogs were big. That much I knew with certainty, and the image in my mind was of an Alsatian, a German shepherd. I have never owned a dog, never had a pet of any kind, but I have never been afraid of them either. That's the thing with animals, and it may be the same with us humans, too. Fear is contagious. A person backs away, begins to act erratically, and the dog senses it. Then it too will become afraid, uneasy, which is when things are liable to take a turn for the worse.

One of them was loose and seemed to have little interest in me, instead sniffing about the ground a meter or so to my left. The other came straight for me, a few quick strides and then its heavy paws pressed down on my shoulders. Sitting as I was, I kept my head bowed and felt his snout sniffing at my forehead. Its mouth wide open an inch or so from my nose, my nostrils filling with the musky smell of its quick sharp breathing.

I guess the two men wanted to see what would happen, hoping that I would recoil in fear or that the two dogs would attack me, and then they might be able to watch a little: an amusing opening to the day. By that measure, I imagine the whole incident proved to be somewhat of a disappointment. It seems the dogs were quite indifferent to the kafir in the room, even licking me on the nose twice, before their handlers drew them out once more, closing the door firmly behind them.

After that, I had little will to sleep, and in truth little time to do it. Before ten in the morning, the two men returned to move me. Back to the orchard and back to Abu Hamid and, unbeknown to me at the time, back to the place that I would escape from.

CHAPTER 11

Escape

A devoted man, facing many financial hardships in his life, walked into a church one evening. The mass had long ended, and but for him the place was entirely empty. Clasping his hands tightly together, he knelt down at the altar and began to pray. "My Lord. I am a family man," he said. "I have always believed in you and have thus lived a life of goodness, in accordance with your teachings. Yet around me people prosper while I continue to struggle. The bills mount up, and I am no longer confident of meeting my obligations. If you could do me this one favor, I would be very grateful. Please, please, oh please send some luck my way and help me win the weekly lottery. It would be wonderful. It really would."

Happy at having made his request, the man left the church, and for the remainder of that week he eagerly awaited the results of the lottery. But when they came, once again he had failed to win. The Lord is busy, he reasoned, maybe next week. But the next week came and then another and another. Two months passed by, and still he was not the winner.

Somewhat annoyed, the man returned to church. He sat listening to the mass, and then waited for all the parishioners to leave before approaching the altar. "My Lord," he said, "it has been two months since I asked you to assist me in the lottery win and still nothing. Perhaps I was being greedy. It does not have to be the main prize, the second will suffice. Please, please, oh please, it would be wonderful if you could help me. It really would." Confident that his prayers had been heard, the man happily left the church, and proceeded to wait once again for the results of the weekly draw. When he did not win the following week, he thought little of it. Not a problem, next week for sure, but the next week came and went, and another and another.

For six months, the bills continued mounting and the man did not win so much as a penny. Irate, he stomped into church and knelt forcefully down at the altar. "My Lord, why have you abandoned me? I ask this one thing. It would have been wonderful, it really, . . . " he began to say, when a deep voice boomed above him. "It would be wonderful my son, it really would, if you could please, please, oh please, help *me* a little and actually buy a ticket!"

It is an old joke, but there is a lesson in there, one that will always be relevant. It is a common mistake to render faith a state of passive hope, rather than a vehicle for action. Many people have assured themselves that they will find justice, that they will find salvation, by virtue of being Christians, by carrying the name of Christ as a part of their identity. However, that in itself is not sufficient, and anyone who thinks it is has failed to comprehend the teachings of Christianity. *Faith by itself, if it does not have works, is dead.*

When a blind beggar sitting beside the road heard the noise of many going by, and asked them the reason for their gathering, they told him that, *"Jesus of Nazareth is passing by." And he cried, "Jesus, Son of David, have mercy on me!" And those who were in front rebuked him, telling him to be silent, but he cried out all the more, "Son of David, have mercy on me!" And Jesus stopped, and commanded him to be brought to him. And when he came near, he asked him, "What do you want me to do for you?" He said, "Lord, let me receive my sight." And Jesus said to*

him, "Receive your sight; your faith has made you well." And
immediately he received his sight and followed him.

Faith alone would not have delivered this man to what he desired. He had to endure, to insist even when those around him screamed for him to be silent. Faith alone is not enough for *the demons also believe.* We must endeavor, we must *strive to enter through the narrow door.*

Knowing this well, I did not look simply for an immediate reprieve from the horrors of my predicament, for an intervention that would bring about my rescue, or a transaction that would bring about my release, but I also looked for the opportunity to seize the freedom that I so desperately hoped for. On the twenty-third day of my captivity, such an opportunity at long last presented itself.

After the incident with the dogs in the small rectangular room, the two men returned that afternoon and, in keeping with the regular procedure, loaded me into the car, this time on the backseat carpet, and transported me once again to the orchard.

With the prospect of release in exchange for payment diminishing, I found my spirits sinking further on that day. For all the promises, assurances, and, at times, kind encouragement, there was little new to break the repetition of the loop in which I had found myself. And what few additions there were, in fresh threats, beatings, and a growing lack of care for my physical well being, only served to make my prospects gloomier. It was difficult not to feel as though I were circling the drain of an inevitable conclusion. The only partly uplifting development came in the "Al Salaam Alaikum" of the man waiting to receive me, which I immediately recognized as the voice of Abu Hamid.

Wordlessly, they led me onward for a short distance, just far enough so that I was alone without ever being unattended. There I sat, while they moved away and spoke a little.

Obviously, I could not know what was soon coming, and still I wonder, if I had known, what things I might have done differently to prepare. What I did was sit there, gently scratching at my wrists, at the points where the metal of the cuffs chafed against the rawness of the skin beneath. They had placed them on too tight, these men, behind my back, as was the custom most times when I was being transferred, and I hoped that once they left, it would be myself and Abu Hamid only, so he could move my hands to the front and loosen the handcuffs a little. That was all I wanted. No great planning. No moving the pawn an innocent distance while the rook and knights lay waiting. Just a minor upgrade in comfort. So when the men did eventually leave, and several minutes had passed by, that was what I requested.

"Are you doing ok?" he had kindly asked, already fumbling with the key to move my hands forward.

"I am alright, as good as can be," I said, feeling relief when the cuff around my left wrist opened and the handcuffs dangled from my right. I stretched my shoulder as I moved my hands around to the front, holding them palm up. "If you could though . . ." I began to ask, "They are very tight and it's getting quite painful, so if you could please loosen them a little."

"Alright," he said without hesitation, turning the key inside the lock, hooking in a finger, and pulling out to a series of clicks. "Better?" he asked.

"Yes," I nodded, feeling immediately more comfortable. "Thank you."

"Umm, alright, I am going to go get some food," he said. "I will be back shortly."

I am not sure why he told me that. I guess he was not thinking. It is just what you do when you leave someone, and there are only the two of you present. You say where you are headed and how long you are going to be. Abu Hamid walked away, and while I sat there waiting, I began to slowly rotate my wrists, to ease the stiffness of such a lengthy period of constrained movement.

Still with no greater plans, with no thoughts beyond that simple action. It was in the next part that it began.

When I lay my hands down onto my lap, I felt the metal slide down farther, farther than I was used to, almost beyond the wrist, to the beginning of my thumb. Unthinking, and in the moment, I looped my left hand under, grabbing at the chain with my fingers, and began to pull my right hand back and back, and harder, feeling the metal slowly slide, scraping on the bone, that sharp pinch of the skin at the point of tearing, and then, just like that, no pain. It was off.

I drew a breath. My pulse suddenly quickening. And the thoughts began forming.

Nudging the blindfold up a little, I moved to the other wrist. With one hand free to operate, I was now able to see. My sight, though unfocused at first, was quickly adjusting, and I began to push and pull. Tucking in my thumb and pressing harder. It was seconds. Another pinch of pain, and then relief. They were off.

Everything was done in seconds.

Decide.

A glance backward. No one there. Flat field and rows of palm trees in the distance.

I have to. My heart racing faster. If they see me, I die. Absolutely they will shoot me, and with good reason.

Decide.

Now or never. *Do it. Do it.*

I yank the blindfold from my eyes, and take off running, kicking off my shoes before my bare feet start pounding on the ground beneath them. *God give me strength and energy.*

Running where?

The words are rushing through my mind, like billboards I am speeding past on an empty highway. *"The air is nice here,"* Abu Hamid had said. *"It is because of the river."*

Onward I run, breathing hard, one breath coming straight after the other. Wanting so very much to turn around, to look behind me, to know if he is back, if he can see me. No use in that. *Faster.*

What do you hear? The man had asked.

I can hear the water running.

This is where we end them.

The water. It has to be this way. I race ahead. I think I can hear it. *God, please guide me.* My legs tiring. Acid spilling through the muscles. Molten hot and seizing, and I hear it. Surely. The water up ahead!

Trees and grassless earth. I slow down, stepping through it. Hands out, dancing side to side, the soles of my feet taking the worst of it. Through the shadows, to the sun and to the river. And there it is. The Tigris, twenty meters ahead of me.

A quick glance, and I see no one. No time to pause.

Breathlessly, I bound forward. In tight crowds, bunches and bunches of dirty yellow straw stand tall in the water, lining the banks of the river. Without a hint of slowing down, three steps and I leap into them. The water is both cold and warm, in the way that water can be when you first dip inside it. Kneeling, legs tucked beneath me, I turn, wrapping my fingers around the straw to steady myself, and cast a long stare all around me. Nothing. No people. No sounds of anyone calling. Only the water rushing and my own deep breathing. Ominously I turn again, looking to the other side, but I am too far in to see it clearly. If I were higher, it would be easier to tell. The water swooshes on, and I can feel the strength of the current pushing. Such power. *God give me strength*.

Around two hundred meters. That's the width by my rough measure. That is the strait of my journey.

I can do it, I quickly think. Swatting away all arguments to the contrary. That I have not had a proper meal for twenty-four days. That my back, hips, arms, and legs are all bruised and beaten. That it has been years since I have weighed so little, since I have been so weak and immobile. All true, and yet none of it matters. These are the moments absent of choice. Where we can break the rules of reason.

I unclasp the straw and push forward. Arms rotating to the side, legs kicking back behind me. Endeavoring to keep on moving, propelled by fear and desperation. The first full swallow of water fills my mouth, and I tilt my head to avoid it. Still so very close, I am conscious of staying low, not too visible. Soon they will be coming, they will search for me, bullets at the ready.

Onward. My mind is clearing. Alive only in the here and now. This is all that matters. Each second is everything. My whole life purely in the moment. Twenty meters. It is hard to tell, and I will not turn to verify it. Eyes low. There is only water. Bluish brown and rushing, a herd in the midst of migrating. For every meter gained, I am moving five downriver. Such is the current, and I am thankful for it. No matter what obstacles it adds, it gives more in its assistance. Away is best, no matter the direction.

Fifty meters. A quarter of the way, and I feel myself tiring. *So soon!* Every movement slows, the river seemingly rising, my head bobbing farther under, and for longer. I draw a breath and splutter out gulps of water and my own saliva. *Drop your arms down lower. Steady strokes. Keep them constant.* Onward, slow but continuing. The negative thoughts begin to jostle to the fore. *It's too far, you are too weak*, they whisper.

Sixty. Seventy. I labor on. No choice. No turning. *God be with me.* I have known this before. Everyone has. When the power all but drains out of you. When you are running, and your energy is spent, when you have lifted a weight repeatedly and there is nothing left in you, when the next ten meters seem to be a mile, and that weight you could have flung an hour earlier now seems nailed to the ground. A hundred meters, halfway across the river, and it is all but over.

I have struck it, the invisible wall you cannot scale and I cannot turn from. My head is woozy, and it is all I can do to simply stop from going under. Every effort is dedicated to that. No longer am I moving forward. The sound of my breaths has faded. Only the roar of the river surrounding me. It is as though I am becoming a part of it, floating in the center of its mouth as it prepares to swallow me.

I have read some people who say that there is peace in such moments, a warmth inside the darkness, almost inviting your surrender. And I guess there were flickers of that for me. Truly, I had tried. Not just in the escape but through all of it. To then die, not by a sword or a bullet. Well, there was something in that.

Maybe something better. And still there came the tearful thoughts: What of my mother? What of my brothers and sisters? I would be gone, and they would never know the truth of me washed up on some riverbank, along with all the faceless others. *The water is no good anymore*, the man had said, *too much blood, too many bodies*. It was coming in snapshots. Blinking pictures. The ones that tether us to life. I guess that's what people mean when they say their lives flashed before them. It isn't the story of all your moments. It is the stripping of the unnecessary. The foregoing of the unneeded. It is the summoning of the final strength within us, grasping on to what we are least willing to relinquish, those many fragments of love.

Black.

I am going under.

And then up again. A startled breath wheezing through the corners of my mouth.

Black.

And up again.

Every fresh breath chokes me, my lungs filling with water. The current is too strong, and I am too weak. There is too far to go, and I can barely keep from sinking under. Back again, I slide and every time I do, it seems as though I am lifted. Every time I dip, craning my head back to bite a chunk of air to take with me, the bright sun shining down in yellow blotches on my eyes before dimming, every time somehow, I rise again. As though a hand, unseen from out of the depths, reached up in assistance. I was dying, but death would not take me.

For the passing of some minutes, there I stay, locked in a seesaw of survival. *Come on. Try.* Then suddenly, as fast as I can, I peel my sodden shirt off my body, kick off my trousers, and, in my pants and vest, I start up again. The rest is a blur.

Time is not a constant tick, and here was another set of seconds. Time's magic trick. Long, so very long and yet almost non-existent. As though the seconds were being pulled so hard and stretched so far that they grew too thin for eyes to see them. The slowest half hour of my life passed by without my having any of it safe in my memory, just the ache of knowing it took place. And when it ended, somehow I had crossed safely to the other side.

Lines of straw again filled the bank of the river, and I rested in the safety of their disguise. In a state beyond exhaustion, I dipped down low, until the water lapped up on my chin; closed my eyes; and simply stayed there for a while. Waiting for the breaths to return to a level of constancy, for my balance to return to me, for my mind to think of what to do next.

The river was deep along this bank, and even though I was close to shore my legs were still unable to touch the bottom. The straw was useful then, for cover and equally for support. That, along with the strength and direction of the current, meant that I could continue to drift downstream with relative ease. The plan was to get as far away as possible, and there was little else to it. I could not know exactly where I would find myself, or what choices might eventually come my way. Instead, I thought only of two objectives. To cover more ground, and not to be seen.

When the skies above began to dim, and the evening began to descend, I heard the first echoes of them calling. The faint sound of words, shouted, at times to one another, and at other times to me, sentences punctuated with the pop of gunfire. "Where?" the word would fly, like fireworks being set off, before the boom that swiftly follows. "I see him," they would say, and fire again. I guess it was a ploy to lure me out, to make me panic and give away my position.

By my estimation, it had been around three in the afternoon when I had first jumped into the water. As the stars began to shine, and all around slid back to blackness, some six odd hours must have passed with me inside that river, and something stranger than tiredness crept over me. I shivered from the cold and cooling water, and felt as though my skin were absorbing it. That the moisture was sinking through the flesh and down to the bone, and my whole body sagged under the weight of it. Leaving was not an option. The hour was not late enough for that. Clad only in my underwear, and soaked from head to toe, I could not run through such treacherous surroundings. At a hopeful guess,

I had moved four or so miles downriver, yet these were still some of the most dangerous territories in Iraq, and perhaps the world. Instead I reached for the straw and moved farther inside its protection. That and the near darkness should offer me time to rest, I reasoned.

However, I would soon learn otherwise.

It was no more than minutes before the first sound perked up my attention. I only half heard it at first, and wondered if it was an illusion brought about by my fright and paranoia. And then agonizing seconds, when I became absolutely still, waiting in breathless anticipation. Before I heard the noise again, and a morbid dread fell over me. People. Not simply walking by but searching. Not on the other side of the river but somewhere beside me. Close, and moving closer.

Careful not to give away my location, I ducked deeper into the water, holding tight to the straw to steady myself and reduce the need to move. I so wanted to see, to discover where they were, but it seemed foolish to try.

God help me.

It is just a flicker, but I see it. A beam of light passing across the water, darting to the banks. They are moving right toward me.

"No," says one. It is the first word I heard clearly. He repeats it, and the sound grows louder.

Pass me by. Pass me by.

There is more than one. All walking meters from one another. Shining torches. Searching.

"You see him?" they keep asking of each other.

My heart races, but I am barely breathing. No sound. No movement. And suddenly, I hear it, the shrill excitement in his voice piercing through me, "I see him!"

The light strikes me squarely in the eyes, and I turn away squinting. Again he shouts, the winner of their treasure hunt. "There he is. I see him. There he is."

The blindfold is off, but I lower my eyes and I am momentarily back to the solitary influx of noises. Hurried footsteps.

The others rushing over. "Don't you move!" he screams. "Stay right there." More lights. More people. One steps, leaning in for a better look, the lights shimmying quickly up and down as he loses his footing on the bank. "Don't you move. Right here I will put a bullet in you." It may be the same person shouting. I cannot tell. "I will kill you right there in the water."

It's almost comical. All I want is to step out of the water. To not have to hold on, to not have to move my legs and grip on to the straw to stop myself from sinking. All I want to do is step out of the water onto the ground, and fall over.

Soon a crowd has gathered. Most are standing a distance away, just watching. I glance upward, and the first thing I see, beyond the silhouette of legs and arms, is the gun the man is holding, and pointing loosely in my direction.

"Get him out," he orders, and three step over to the edge of the river, hands out for me to grab onto. I pull on the straw, move slowly toward them, and with a heave they draw me out.

They take a step back, and I stand there. Shivering cold and surrounded, when a man suddenly strikes me forcefully across my ear and to the back of my neck. I come close to falling but steady myself. Head bowed, not wanting to see them. There are people from the village here, all come to see what is happening. All around me I hear them, whispering to one another, their stares pressing up against me.

"Where are you from?" the man who struck me asks. "Huh? Those others, why have they taken you?"

"I don't . . ." I begin to answer, my voice trailing off in exhaustion and in anger. Angry at having to explain the barbaric actions of the men who had abducted me, as though I must have been guilty of some wrong for them to do it. As though I must be deserving, when deserve, for quite some time, has had little to do with anything in our country.

"Huh?" through gritted teeth, the man asks once more of me.

"I don't know," I answer. "Why don't you ask them? Why don't you ask them why they want to kill me?"

"You are Nasrani [Christian]," he says, almost as a question.

My legs ache, and I slowly sit down on the ground while they continue to surround me. "Yes. I am Nasrani," I answer, aware that he knows that already.

"You are the people of the book," he says, and I nod wearily. "Why would they take you? This is *haram* [sinful]."

"And why are you telling me this? Huh?" I asked. "Say it to them. Tell them that it is sinful. They are the ones who want to kill me. They want to kill me, and so I ran."

He had no answer to that, or at least none that he was willing to share with me. The clearest symptoms of a land where justice and righteousness have lost their way are the screaming words that remain unspoken. How else can men dare to flog the value of humanity before the eyes of its people. Silence is the cruelest sound for those who need it to be broken.

In whispers, they spoke to one another after that, and it seemed that we were all there waiting.

CHAPTER 12

Beyond Survival

Another trapdoor in time. The humming sound of a small propeller in the water. Sitting there, cold, barely dressed in anything at all, surrounded by guns and people, I heard the noise of the boat approaching, and knew that they had come for me. The escape, the exhaustion, the fear, the attempt to save my life; it wasn't that it was all for nothing, but that it was far worse. I had disobeyed and been captured. What would come next?

As ever, there was the fear of the Americans watching. That they might be monitoring this stretch of river, where a number of people had suddenly thought to gather at ten at night, and so we carried on waiting. They pushed the boat up to the bank, and the three men who climbed out stood close among those who had caught me.

Like an offending student sitting alone in the hallway, readying himself for what is coming while the principle discusses the punishment with his parents, I sat on the ground, eyes low, as a few meters away they spoke in hushed tones. One side was no doubt telling the tale of what I had done, while the other described how they had found me.

I am not sure what made them feel sufficiently safe from the curious eyes of the American army, but after a half hour or so had passed, they loaded me into the boat, the three of them climbing aboard with me. They said their goodbyes to the villagers, yanked the engine back to life, and off we went across the river.

All the hours I had spent inside that water, my face pressed so close to death and back again, toiling to pay for every meter gained. All those efforts in a matter of minutes had been undone to nothing. The boat slowed as it pushed into the long straw of the riverbank, and I had returned to where I started.

With his hand pressed against the back of my neck, keeping my head bowed, one man led me out while the other two secured the boat behind us. A part of me thought it would be over then and there, just as they had said before. "This is where we end them." But onward we marched. A short brisk walk, his hand on my neck throughout out, pushing, my legs peddling fast to keep pace, trying not to fall over, until we reached the waiting minivan.

The door was already open. "Enter!" he growled, his closed fist pounding at the base of my skull before I tumbled forward. I do not how many were there, but it seemed many had searched for me. The car was full, people seated on either side. With my heavy head bowed between my slumping shoulders, I crouched down in the empty space in the middle, and that was when I felt it. A hand laid gently atop my head. It stayed there unmoving for a few brief seconds before it drew away.

Instantly I knew who it was. Abu Hamid, who could not speak to me with words just then, had laid his hand onto my head instead. And I heard him, without a sound I heard him ask, *Why would you do this? Don't you see what you have done? Not just to you but to both of us. Don't you see that I can't help you anymore.* I sank a little lower, and in that moment my sorrow was as much for him as for what awaited me.

"We have brought him." The man in the front was speaking on the telephone. "Yes," he said. "They gave him to us. . . . he . . . he is here . . . in the car with us." He grunted, the phone snapping shut in his hand. "Move," he said, and the engine rumbled, the tires squealing before the van rolled forward.

If you were being driven to the gallows, would you wish for a short drive or a long one?

I had not noticed them so much before, maybe a little along the last brisk walk from the river, but it seemed that I had trod on many thorns during some portion of this day. The soles of my feet were covered with them, and each shake of the car made them throb with pain.

When the drive evened out a little, and the flat road served to hush the sounds of the van in motion, the man upfront turned back to me. I could not see, but I heard the rustling of his movement.

"How did you cross the river?" he quite suddenly asked, as though the question had been inside him all along, and he could contain it no longer.

"I swam," I answered, and my voice seemed small, croaking its way out of my throat.

"You swam?" he skeptically repeated.

"Yes," I said, "I crossed it swimming."

"You swam. Well, we will see. For sure we will see."

With all that was on my mind, I guess it is no surprise that it had yet to occur to me, but I now knew what he was thinking. To cross the river would be no easy task. The water is deep, and the current is stronger than someone would imagine before finding himself inside it. A fit and able man would struggle to complete such an endeavor. So considering the state I was in, it was easy to understand the disbelief of my captors. And there were other issues too, such as how I had found the river, and, more importantly, how I had come to remove the handcuffs.

When Abu Hamid placed his hand on my head, he did so not only in reprimand, but in a quiet request for help.

As the van slowed to a stop, dread was bubbling up inside of me. I had been subjected to repeated rounds of horror, from the chaos of the abduction; to fear of needing the bathroom, and the consequences of such a need going unattended; to the surprise of the initial beating, and the fear that it would be a continuing occurrence; to the first time I believed a particular moment might truly to be my last. I had learned that identifying specific fears was a means of overcoming them. As they removed me from the van, I wondered whether I was afraid of death. Of pain. Or of enduring.

With the wall firmly behind me, outside a small house, I crouched down on the dusty ground. The hand of a man remained, pressed firmly down on my neck, fixing my eyes on my knees, even though I had no intention of raising them. No blindfold and no handcuffs. There was little need for them. A tired, unarmed man surrounded by ten angry others and the guns they carried.

The door opened, and out he came. His walk was much the same as that of the men who had entered my room that day with sticks in hand. Not hurried so much as purposeful. Already knowing what he wished to do before he did it.

"Why would you escape?" he asked, and as he did, the other man lifted his hand from my neck and the whip came crashing. I fell forward, down on my knees and elbows, and before I could rise a little, or even put out a hand for cover, I felt the cable rip across my bare back once more, and again and again. There was no stopping him then. With every twist, he whipped the cable down with as much power as he could muster. And every time it struck me, the pain worsened, the old cuts and bruises opening at this fresh assault. "Don't you know we are going to kill you?" through gritted teeth he screamed, while the hits continued falling. And with every fall of the cable, with every slice of skin, my body jerked and my mouth bit out and found the air empty. And still he continued, until I no longer wondered when he would stop and instead felt my consciousness fading. It was then that the strikes began to slow, the continuous blows reduced to splutters, his energy and hatred having ebbed to enable only single strikes, and then finally none. "Take him inside," he ordered, and two men, one on either side, dragged me to a dark little room and dropped me there, the door closing after me.

There would be another visit that night; I do not know how long after. In fact, I did not notice them until they stood hovering over me, a trick of light, moving shadows in the darkness. You cannot tell what you saw in such states, only that you saw something. And in forgetting to look down, in forgetting not to stare, I turned to it for that second when the first strike of the cane ripped across my back. It was one of *those* beatings, unaccompanied by demands that I convert. No why would you do such a thing. Nor any why can you not see what will have to happen. This visit was a part of the happening, and I did not protest. I did not have enough breath to waste on empty words to those who had no thought to listen. The insults fell with the strikes, and I could not but lie on the ground collecting them. Through it all, with every swipe of the cane, as I felt the hand of death draw closer, my only thought was, *If this is it, my Lord, then I am ready.*

When the men grew tired or satisfied, or both, one threw a pair of jogging trousers on the ground beside me, and the other knelt down, pulling my limp arms behind my back, clicking the cuffs shut, and tying the blindfold tightly across my eyes.

They left me then, but before they did, as the door was closing, the one man said, "Wait until tomorrow. Tomorrow, you will meet your destiny."

So be it. The following morning, I was already awake and in the midst of my prayers when the two returned to me.

The room was small, and I had moved to the other side of it. The injuries were mounting and comfort, which had long been a relative term, had in these past days increased in volatility. Seeking relief was like tinkering with the volume of a television, without ever gaining control of it. I would move in cautious inches. The noise lowering. Inch by inch. Afraid that the next movement might send it soaring. And when the position could be held and the volume became tolerable, I would remain as still as could be, until the next unexpected reverberation stirred me. With the blindfold on, hands cuffed behind me, I was nestled in the corner, as far away from the door as possible. As they stepped inside, my back instinctively straightened, and I winced at the pain of it.

Mumbling the conclusion of my morning prayer, I said a quiet and fitting amen as the men strode toward me, the sticks rattling in their hands. All my thoughts were suddenly flooded with the echo of the last word they had uttered, "destiny."

"Move," the one man ordered. Without giving me even a semblance of time to comply, his hand hooked beneath my arm to drag me forward. On my knees, I shuffled with him to the center of the little room where the first whack of the stick would find me. Landmines. My back exploded in pain, and I tensed up in expectation of the incoming flurry of blows. But he stopped. This would be no ordinary beating. They had come with a task. A need for answers.

"You," he said, his husky voice garbling up the word in disgust at the worthlessness of the *you* he referred to, "you are going to tell us the truth, every part of it. Do you understand?" And then the next strike landed. That was the way it would be. The hits falling down like question marks at the end of each sentence, serving both to keep my attention from wavering and to shake off whatever doubts I might have as to the real consequences of noncompliance.

"I understand," I said.

"We will kill you, right here, in this room. Do you understand?"

"I understand!" I cried as the next hit fell and the pain intensified.

I knew the question he would ask, and my stomach still sank at the sound of it.

"How did you get across the river?"

There would be no avoiding this.

"I swam."

A strike. From the other side. They had slipped into their roles, the one asking the questions and the other dolling out the punishment.

"Don't you lie to me!" he screamed. "How did you cross that river?"

"Why would I lie?" I asked, rushing the words out to stave off the next blow. "You all saw me. I was soaked. I was in the water."

"How did you cross?"

Two hits. The second harder than the first, and I slumped forward, pulling my cuffed arms up behind me so they could blunt the next strike from landing squarely on my back. "How did you cross?" he said. But when I tried to speak, the words became stuck as the breath was rasping out of me. And when they did come, they rang louder than I had intended.

"I am not lying!" I said. "The guard. He had gone. Left to do something, and when he walked away . . . I heard him walk, heard that he had gone, and I ran, I ran toward the sound of the river, and when I reached it, I jumped in."

"And you swam across?"

"Yes," I said, at once relieved that his question did not come with the accompanying blow. "It took a long time, but yes, slowly I swam to the other side."

"Who. Helped. You?" he asked, as though I had yet to grasp the true purpose of his questions, and with that the stick thudded down again.

"No one. I was alone. Like I said . . ." my voice trailed off as the next hit fell.

"And your handcuffs? Huh? They just fell from your wrists?"

"No, I pulled them off." And the thought suddenly came to me, the only piece of evidence I had to corroborate my story. "Look at my wrists!" I shouted, arching my hands from behind my back. "Uncuff me, and I will show you."

Two again. This time from the man with the questions. "You lie!" he said, as though insulted by the fact that I would presume to try and fool him, "The guard, he helped you, don't you lie to me?"

"He did not help me! Look at my hands. Look at the cuts where I pulled them off."

Then the stick whipped down again, cracking my elbows, and he screamed his threats. "We will kill you both. You and him, the both of you." I felt a rush of exasperation envelope me. For all this time, I had endured for myself, for my beliefs, for my God, and for my religion. This man would not die because of my actions.

"You want to kill me?" I asked. "Do it. I am not afraid of it, and I have no reason to lie. But if you kill that guard, then you kill an innocent man. One of your own."

"Our own huh?"

"Yes. An innocent man and a Muslim."

"And you?"

"Me? You will do what you will do."

"And you will not become a Muslim?"

"No. I will not," I said. I was done with any kind of bargaining, with giving them hope that they might convert me. If that ever truly had been their intention. "*You* are the ones who need to understand something," I said, as I felt the blood dripping from my shoulder. "I will not become a Muslim, and I fully know that you are going to kill me for it."

There would be no more questions and no more strikes. Not just then anyhow. The two men walked away, and I shuffled slowly back to the corner of that little room, trying to find some balance of comfort.

There is a gift in this world that most people will receive at only one time, and no other. For this most precious gift lies beyond the blackest black, where you begin to see a glint of a warm and unfamiliar light shining, there it is found, resting on the moving boots of death. Just as all those years ago I had walked into a church looking for one thing and had left with quite another, so too did I sit inside the darkness of that room, my eyes closed and staring out with a different vision.

We live in a world filled with distractions. With petty wants passing themselves off as needs, and fleeting joys masquerading as fulfillment. If there is a gift to be found in the close proximity of death, then it is surely perspective. Whether you are one who believes, as I do, and did in that moment, that soon you will be in conversation with your creator, or whether you are one who believes that you will simply reach life's conclusion, you cannot but look to measure the substance of yourself and of your hours in that moment. You cannot but ask, who could I have been in this world? And who was I truly?

With regret, I stared at the many failures of my life, at the times when I could have done more but chose not to. The people I could have helped but, for whatever unworthy reason, chose not to. The sick, the poor, the lonely. Through the blindfold, I watched a projector play my memories, and found myself too often quick to judge. At times too ready to exclude, too unwilling to understand, too slow to forgive.

For me, and for those who believe as I do, the purpose of life is to find a oneness with God. There lies true happiness. And yet the quest for happiness can never be a selfish endeavor, for being one with God means to dwell in the collective and not the singular. Not to believe in heaven, and perform the necessary acts to reach it, but to believe in love and in living a life in accordance with that purpose. Even they who do not love in the name of God will have the love of God beside them. The shadow of death purifies this belief. It blows away the dust of the unimportant, and though it is neither a controversial nor a novel thought to say that love is the ultimate measure of a life well lived, to stand beside your scales and to weigh the acts of *I did* against the ones of *I should have done* is to learn once and for all that the measure of life is meaning.

Once such an outlook has been realized, then one has crossed the threshold of that most basic instinct of all living things—survival. They could not break me. The threat of that had disappeared. I had known it with the utmost certainty, and somehow when the Chair Man came to see me the following day, he too had grown convinced of it.

When you are thirsty, as I commonly was during those days, you can push the urge away for a while by busying yourself with other thoughts, with anything unassociated with drinking.

I would think of specific occasions, certain events, or certain days, and I would watch them, toying with the malleability of time, pausing and playing them in slow motion. I would concentrate on the intricate details. The watch a person wore. Or the colors of a painting I had seen: the brown-green of a blade of grass, the sweep of a brushstroke. This technique is a means of escaping, of pushing away the inconvenient wanting, but the thirst never strays far, and always it returns a little stronger.

I was sitting with my back straight and still, my legs crossed beneath me, my cuffed arms as relaxed as I could make them, considering they were dangling behind my back to the floor, as I flipped slowly through the pictures in my mind. When the door opened, I did not move. It could have heralded another beating, another round of interrogation, but the sound was different. The steps this time were less urgent.

"Ha, how are you?" the Chair Man asked, without a hint of irony.

"I am as you see me," I answered.

"And you have not changed your mind?"

"No."

My words came quickly, and I could hear him groaning expectedly. If it had been under any other circumstances I would be tempted to say that I heard him smile.

"I am beginning to think that you are not going to change your mind, are you?" he asked.

"No," I said, and a silence drifted in between us. It was funny to think it, but really what was there to talk about? My mind was made up, and there was very little he could tell me that I would believe. This was a waste of time for both of us.

"It is not just Islam," he finally said, and from the sound of his voice, I sensed he had moved a little farther away from me. "It is a life I am giving you here, to teach, to be a man of use."

"You are a believer, and you don't me need me to tell you." I said, "You know that what you are doing here is wrong."

"It is not wrong . . . ," he began to say.

"It is," I interrupted. "I am not a soldier, and you and I, we are not at war. I am a man who helps people. But it really does not matter. I will not change my mind, and I have nothing to fear from any of you. So."

"Well," he said, "there will be a conclusion to this. Soon Inshallah."

I nodded.

"Is there anything you need?" he asked.

"Some water."

"Very well. They will bring some now," he said, and left before I could thank him, though I do not recall if I ever intended to.

When a couple of hours had passed by with me in the room alone and uninterrupted, I presumed that, like all his other promises, the water would go undelivered. At other times, I would simply have called out and asked for it, but in the last days my treatment had deteriorated significantly. The beatings were becoming an everyday affair, and I did not wish to break my solitude if I could at all avoid it. Additionally, I had already told him, and the room service there was not quite as prompt as it could be. So I waited. Thinking I would wait another half hour, and then I would call, but the half hour did not pass before a man entered.

He walked straight to me, and, when he got there, he immediately crouched down, reaching behind me for my wrists, unlocking the cuffs, and cuffing my hands in the front. "How are you?" he asked, as he placed the cup inside my hands, and so surprised was I by the sound of his voice that for a second I once again forgot about the water. "You are back?" I asked.

"Yes," Abu Hamid quietly answered, tilting the cup upward as the liquid poured in. "Drink," he said, and I drew it to my mouth, drinking it all.

"You want some more?" he asked.

"Yes. A little."

Again he poured the water, and, as I drank, he placed a hand on my shoulder and whispered, "They tried to kill me."

"No!" I said. "I told them. I told them you had no part in it. I said you left for a moment, and I ran. That I was alone in what happened."

"I know this," he answered. "I know. Afterward they told me."

"Ok," I said, and he grabbed the cup and left. That would be the last time I ever spoke to him.

CHAPTER 13

Are you not pleased?

What makes one person wish to inflict pain on another? It is a silly question. Of course there are a myriad of reasons—thousands, millions—and an infinite number of circumstances. But are there? Is it not always through some form or combination of wanting? What if we were to exclude the exercise of violence for survival. What would be left? To seek acceptance. To belong. To break free. To become powerful, influential, rich. To bring about justice in a world that the perpetrator believes is out of balance. To drink the elixir of vengeance. To validate oneself. To reach a semblance of happiness, and dare I say to find peace. And of course there are more, and near enough as makes no difference, all the perpetrators of violence point to some outward force that forces their hands to enact such action. Still I cannot but feel that there is a hole in all of us, and the seemingly unexplainable, and utterly undeniable, need to fill it leads us onto a treacherous road filled with pitfalls.

Cables. Not Sticks.

Insults. Not questions.

And anger. Real, visceral anger. On the twenty-sixth day of my captivity, at some point in the late morning hours, two men entered the room and instantly got to the business of carrying out the beating. Except it was not simply business. It was not free of emotion but sodden with it. I guess it was considered a righteous deed performed to punish the kafir for his offenses, but still I wondered. As the cables swung down through the air lashing my back, and I curled up tight beneath them, drowning in the incessant pain, I wondered how many of the insults were truly meant. Whether these men hated me, and the insults flowed from that emotion, or whether they insulted me to better convince themselves of the hatred. One may ask why it matters? Either way, I was still where I was, still on the ground, still being beaten, still being edged toward the strike that might be the one too many, the one that would cause my body to give out altogether. And yet for me, it made a great deal of difference.

It was a drawn-out beating, among the worst I endured. Not only because the beatings had an accumulative effect, each one opening wounds that were yet to heal, but from the sheer frenzy of it. By the time the last blows fell, I was lying on the floor unmoving, shaking only at the points of impact.

There I remained for quite some time, even after they had left me.

That was the morning, and by the middle of the afternoon, the same two men returned. I had moved by then, with a stinging slowness, back to the corner of the room where the narrowing of the walls could prop me up.

The key rummaged in the lock before it turned and the door swung soundlessly open. My skin itched in apprehension of what was coming, but I remained unmoved, perfectly still until I was ordered to do otherwise. "Stand," he said. And so I did, somewhat gingerly. My hands were moved from the front to the back, and I knew then that we would be leaving. Quietly we walked, out of the little room and the little house to the car, where I was squeezed into the confines of the boot. Then down came the hood, shuddering at the hinges.

From the words of the Chair Man, expressing his growing conviction that my mind would not be altered, I reasoned that the end was near. I thought this drive might in fact be the journey to the place of execution. Fear is an involuntary reaction. People can talk themselves out of it; they can calm their nerves and apprehension. However, it is far easier to do when the fear is irrational. I was no longer afraid that they would break me, yet still I feared. Still there stirred that struggle inside of me, that recoiling from the waves of torture and the heat of uncertainty. As the car continued for a lengthier time than was customary, it became increasingly harder for me to subdue the worry from boiling over.

For an hour we drove, with me rattling about inside the boot, before the car came to a quite sudden stop.

Those were slow seconds. Where everything became louder. Where I grew annoyed at the sound of my own breathing, where I wanted to shush myself so I could better listen. Better hear where we were: Were there other cars? Were other people coming from their homes to greet my captors?

I strained to listen simply for the point of knowing, for the need to feel some sense of control, even if it were false. In reality, if I had been able to decipher where we were, beyond its being some unknown road or home, what could I have done with the information?

The car doors opened, one and then instantly the other. Footsteps on soft ground, muffled in the dirt, and then the boot popped and the air became plentiful. I moved my head up a little, preparing for them to reach in and grab me, to take me to wherever we happened to be, but the man's fist thumped against my temple. There was nowhere for me to move, no give in this shallow space, and he proceeded to pummel me. All the while he shouted his insults. "You son of a bitch!" he spit out between his punches. "Listen up you dog, I am going to call your family, and you will speak with them. You hear me?" he asked, but before I could reply, his fist crashed against my cheek.

Had I heard him correctly? My family?

The thoughts rushed in on me. Could it be? All at once I was light headed, confused, in pain, and excited. The phone began to beep in his hand. Somewhere to the left above me. I heard the dial tone, and he drew away, not far, close enough for me to listen. He wanted me to listen.

"This dog, we are going to kill him, you hear me?" he was shouting and I could not hear the voice on the other end, only that of the man above me, only the stream of threats and insults tumbling from his mouth. "We are going to butcher him, you understand? You want to hear him? You want to hear his voice? Here listen," and he suddenly leaned in toward me, pressing the phone to my ear and holding it there.

"Are you Saad?" asked the voice on the other end, and my heart leaped to hear it. For all my life I had known that voice. My brother Ardwan. "Saad?" he asked again.

"Yes, habibi, it is me."

"Should we pay the money?"

They were after ransom. All this time and still they bargained for more money.

"Pay them," I said, "and when I am out I will take care of things."

"Alright," replied Ardwan. "How are you?"

"I am good," I answered, and as I did, the man ripped the phone away with one hand and punched me with the other. "You are good?" he screamed. "He is not good."

That was the last I heard of the conversation. Hurriedly he stepped away, and I was pushed back down before the car boot slammed above me.

The way back was shorter. Much of the delay must have been intended for effect, to confuse me. An hour's drive did not mean we were an hour away from our starting place. And this was even more the case when they were waiting for a phone call. The two times they had gotten me to speak to someone, first the patriarch and now my brother, had taken place after a lengthy drive that eventually ended beside a silent road. A precaution against tracking the phone signal perhaps. I did not know, but there seemed to be a pattern, and I suspected that I was not the first man, and would certainly not be the last, to be used as cargo for their deal making.

After about thirty minutes or so, we had returned. At least it seemed that way. After being taken from the car and dumped back in the room, I could not tell with certainty. My hands had remained cuffed behind my back, and I could not lift the blindfold to inspect my surroundings. The ground felt the same, bare cement, chipping away in places. And when I moved back blindly, searching for the corner, there it was where I had left it.

The time was early evening when I sat quietly filtering through the possibilities. Another ransom was going to be paid. That much I knew. In all likelihood, it would happen either that night or early the following morning. I had told my brother to pay it knowing that the odds of success were slim. What is the value of money in such circumstances? That is the thought that fuels this ugly business.

I did not know how much my brother would pay, and there was obviously no chance to ask him. However much it was, I would take care of it if I were given the chance, but I was not optimistic. Why would they release me? Perhaps that phone call was the only reason I had not been killed already. The evidence my family needed for surety, after the passing of long days and nights. What would happen once they paid?

I tried to place myself in the minds of my captors. The ones who did not consider my life worth living. At great pains, I had avoided catching glimpses of them. I did not know who they were and how anyone could find them. Yet was it unreasonable for them to suspect otherwise? Perhaps I had seen something, a face I could describe, a name I could remember, some landmark I could identify, anything they might consider posed a danger to them. When dealing with life and death, caution is of the utmost importance. The more I thought about it, the stronger the case for killing me became.

A strange claustrophobia wrapped its hands tighter and tighter around my neck as I weighed each possibility. I had defied them. I had run away and been captured. How could they let me live after that? How could they be sure that I had not seen enough in the hours when I was free to lead the Americans directly to them? The truth was they could not.

Unchecked hope can be a weakness to the man who holds no sway in the outcome. As the beatings intensified, I had mentally walked myself to the door of death so I would be ready when it opened. Those few words from my brother, hearing a living voice from outside this daily nightmare, had pulled me back across the blades of longing. Longing to be at home, to see the faces of my family. To wrap my arms around my mother and tell her that all is well, that she need not worry. To stand once more inside my church, telling all that we must carry on regardless. I longed to be far from here, to hear the door open and not wince at what might be coming.

A lot of people had seen me. Many along the river bank, and in the varying places I was taken. Killing me would intensify the situation. *You are important,* the Chair Man had said in those first few days. Would killing me not come with consequences? And yet the American army had known who I was, and where I was, and still they had chosen not to save me. That thought was one that would not leave me.

I sat in the dock while two lawyers quarreled in my mind, and the only conclusion I could reach was that if they did not release me the following day, be it in the morning or at nightfall, then there would be no release for me at all. This call, this call for ransom, had reset the timer for the brief and final trial.

As the new day dawned, and I chose to stop chasing sleep, the falling sand in the hourglass was a constant in my thinking. The final episode had begun, and if I were to wake once more inside this place, then the grains would surely all have fallen. Be it the end or not, this was a day of prayer.

By midday there had been little movement. A man, one unknown to me, had come and given me water. No unnecessary words had been exchanged between us. The drink had been tipped slowly into my mouth, as my hands were still cuffed behind my back. Then he had left again.

I was alone. Here time was a mixture of smooth and coarse. I wanted the ground to open up and drain away all the awful minutes of waiting, and yet I needed far more minutes than the day could afford to give me.

An hour edged itself along, passed, and then the next began. I listened for sounds and found myself flinching at any whisper of noise. At anything that signified a change. The hum of a car engine somewhere in the distance. The creak of a door opening. People talking. However, the noises I heard were not necessarily what they seemed. The wind masqueraded as an engine, the old structure as the opening of the door. Whatever the source, the faintest sounds triggered my undivided attention, until the volume of false alarms blurred the lines between one reality and another.

When in late afternoon a car arrived and stopped beyond the walls of my cell, my hope was once again ignited, but time dragged on and nothing came of it. A change in the guards perhaps.

By the evening, I was back to measuring the probable against the possible. The possible that filled me with joy and ignited the kind of energy for which there is no physiological explanation, and the probable, with its two wet fingers pinching at the flame of a candle. I thought of them, heard the half seconds hiss by, and watched the wispy stream of smoke rise and disappear altogether.

My Lord . . . if this is the end for me. The purpose. That I should have endeavored to escape without success, that I will never again see the many people whom I love in this life, that mine is the path to martyrdom, then know that I am ready. You have galvanized my heart with love, and no amount of witnessed wickedness can hope to corrode it. I do not wish for death. Quite the opposite. I am afraid, and yet no fear can ever persuade me to trade temporary falsehoods for the lasting truth of who I am with you beside me. If this is the end, my Lord, then I am ready for it. However, if there is more. If the road I travel in this world stretches onward. If there are days to be lived, and work not yet completed. If your purpose for me is not yet done. Then now is the time for something. For a change. A chance. Know that I am grateful for all that you have given me, and I stand ready for the outcome of these days, whatever it may be.

The hours crept on by. The night flowed in, matured, and ebbed on its way to completion. Beneath my veil, I sat and felt it all in gentle tremors, vibrations in the pockets of air around me. Minute by minute, I sat and bore witness to the day and the night, and by all odds, the remnants of my chances fading with the dawn of the following morning.

The light shone in, crawling beneath the door, and from any place that was not blocked completely, filling the room and lightening the blackness visible through the half-inch opening in my blindfold. It was then that I fell asleep, quite suddenly and without warning. I could not tell how much time had passed before a sudden noise stirred me.

My heavy eyelids pried apart in the shaded dark and quickly closed. *It is nothing.*

And then it was there again.

The distant voice of my waking self grew louder, calling me from my rest, *Someone is here,* it said, and I hesitated at the edge of sleep, waiting.

A sound. Talking. Men outside my door and inside the building. Guards? The metal of the key scratched at the lock, and I was awake when the Chair Man entered.

"Good morning," he said.

"Good morning," I answered, shuffling up straight where I was sitting, feeling the pain skip along my spine.

He paced silently. I heard his steps and those of two others who had come with him. He was close, and they were farther off, beside the door. The seconds passed in silence. If he were waiting for me to speak, then he would be waiting for some time longer.

"We are going to release you," he finally said.

I did not answer.

"Did you hear me? We are going to release you. Today."

I heard the words, and still I remained silent. What was there to say to this man? There had barely been a single truth inside the lies he had told me. Why would this be any different?

"Huh?" he took a step toward me. "Are you not pleased?"

"I don't believe you," I said.

"Why?"

"Because you have said it before, and every time you said you would release me, that you have a thing to do, and then . . . well, you keep me here and nothing happens."

"Not this time," he said. "So this is your last chance. Do you not want to stay here? Be free with us?"

"No," I answered. "I do not want to stay here."

"That is it then!" he said abruptly. "Today we will be rid of you."

When he and the two men walked out, I was left alone once more, weighing the words I had heard for the truth of their meaning. *Today. Your last chance. Be free with us. We will be rid of you.*

Rid of me. Today. My journey with these men had reached its conclusion. That much I did believe. Someone would come for me. They would take me from this room. On a long drive no doubt. Then, there would be one of two outcomes. Death or freedom.

CHAPTER 14

The Highway

A motorcycle. I had heard a variety of sounds from the variety of places where I had been confined. This, however, was the first time I had heard the distinctive sputter of a motorcycle engine. The first time I had pinned down the sound of it. Known what it was. It may not have been crucial, but on this day nothing was unimportant. Four-odd hours had passed since the Chair Man's visit. From my learning that today was a day of finality. One way or another.

Since he had left, there had been little to dwell on. No sounds of any comings or goings. I would have known. I had been listening most attentively. And then there was the motorcycle. Its engine louder, at a higher pitch, less even. I heard it sputtering outside, and then the car that soon joined it. At around three in the afternoon, I knew that they had come for me. No doubt about it. For four hours, I had been sitting there waiting for them, but oddly now that they had come, I felt unprepared, as though I were forgetting something. It was the same feeling as when you are waiting to go to the airport, the taxi finally arrives, and you feel that little rush of panic asking you to check again, just one more time, just to be sure you have not forgotten anything. Except I had no bags to pack, nothing to prepare, only the journey.

A door opened. Blurry words. Footsteps. The key, and then they entered.

"Take him up to the car," a man said, I guess both to me and to the others. One on either side, they came to help me stand and I struggled up in compliance. We walked. Out of the house and to the minivan. It was the same kind that had collected me from the river. I knew it because I could see a little as I took the large step up into it, bent legs moving slowly forward, and then down, between the seats. There I knelt, my left shoulder resting against the side of a cushion for some stability.

One man sat close by, with the other two in front. I heard the doors open and close and a seat belt being pulled. As the van engine started, so did the motorcycle's. We moved.

The cycle led the way, and the van followed. Onward we went. With my hands still cuffed behind my back, I struggled to keep my balance through the turns in the road, but it was a far better place to be than the boot, and I was thankful for it. For a half hour we simply drove, with no words from them, neither to me nor to one another. Silence. Just the sounds of the engines, the tires, and metal shaking.

I was tempted to say something. To ask them where we were going. If they were going to grant me my freedom. To tell them that I was assured they were. However, back in my little room I had decided not to, and so I didn't. So much of my captivity had been waiting. A little longer I thought. I would wait a little longer and then I would know.

An hour in and still nothing, when suddenly one of them spoke. It was the man sitting in the back. His question was one of the strangest of any I've ever been asked, or ever will be.

"You don't hate us, do you?"

It took me a second to be sure I had heard him right before I answered. "No," I said. "No, I don't hate any person. My faith asks this of me, to love all people. Even those who harm me.

It's true I don't always accept the things they do, but I don't hate them."

"So if we release you," he said, "you will not inform on us?"

My nerves jangled. I wanted to say a lot, but I didn't. "If you release me," I answered, "I don't think you will ever see my face again."

"Ok," he said, retreating once more into silence.

A little longer, I thought, as the embers of hope began to burn. The minutes ticked by, the car was moving up and down on the bumpy road, and I knelt there waiting. The truth was that even with the deafening thoughts of longing for liberation, I could not shake the question that the man had asked me. He seemed so young, so innocent to begin his question that way. To not simply ask if I would inform on them, but to pin it to whether or not I felt hatred toward them. I could not but pity him.

An hour and a half from the start of our drive, the van slowed to a stop.

"Bring him down," said the man upfront, and I felt a grip beneath my shoulder as I was slowly led outside.

God be with me.

Forward I walked. A man close behind, his hand on the base of my neck. "Enough," said one, and we stopped.

My guide backed away, leaving me there. Standing.

I shook in anticipation. The next words I heard would be the verdict. No more waiting.

"Open his hands," he said, and I pushed them back, trying to be as helpful as possible. The man fumbled with the key until it clicked in place and the cuffs slid open.

"You will not turn around," he ordered, and I nodded in agreement. "Open his eyes." A hand pulled at the knot of the blindfold and it was removed from my face. Cautiously, I opened my eyes, squinting, and saw a long deserted lane ahead, trees on either side.

A hand then moved inside my pocket. He had placed something there.

"This is fifteen thousand dinars," he said. The equivalent of eight dollars. "You walk ahead. You turn around for a second and we will shoot you. Walk and keep walking. In front of you is the highway."

I nodded, and without my making a conscious decision, my legs started moving. Easy steps, I thought, slow and steady. It was all I could do to stop myself from running. I must have been twenty meters down the lane when I heard the roar of the engines, the van and the motorcycle turning, and the blissful fading of sound as they moved away from me. A minute or so, and I was alone. I was truly alone for the only time during my captivity other than my escape. I could no longer hear them, and still I did not turn around, still I simply walked on, my steps quickening.

A strange concentration knotted my stomach. Perhaps disbelief, as though at any moment they would come again, I would hear them calling out, and a gun would pop, sending a bullet whizzing past me.

The lane was long. Nothing but trees. For five hundred meters I walked, searching for the sound of the highway, or any other thing that I would recognize. Time began to drag, and I was conscious of it. These were not areas to be in, especially after dark. I started to jog, but it was difficult because the side of my hip throbbed with pain, and I found myself quickly out of breath and energy. I took it in shifts. Never stopping. A jog and then a walk for rest.

Soon enough I passed the trees and kept walking. There I stared out at barren acres and makeshift lanes. There was nothing familiar to guide me, when suddenly, I saw a building I thought I recognized in the far off distance, an old slaughterhouse for chickens. I thought I knew roughly the area where I was, but I still had no sense of direction. These were tribal lands. Filled with kidnapping gangs and warring rebels. Places that no one would visit unless they absolutely had to. Here I was, a Christian clad in a gray t-shirt that was darkened in places where the blood had dried, dirty jogging bottoms, and sandals. Tired, hurt, and lost. Stumbling about with no identification, only fifteen thousand dinars wadded in my pocket. My level of worry was rising with each passing minute, and all I could think of was the highway, and yet the highway was not enough. What would I do when I got there? The thought jarred my mind and I elbowed it away. It was a challenge for later. My time was dwindling.

A half hour passed and then another. The sun had gone and the blue of the sky was quickly deepening. I jogged along as the panic began to set in. More trees. Nothing but trees and lanes. My head spun, making me nauseated, and I eased back down to a walk. The minutes tumbled by and my movements were slowing. *God help me. I can't be caught again. I won't survive it.*

Looking ahead, I saw a lane bending to the right. It seemed cleaner, as though it had been cleared by common usage. I went to it, taking cautious steps inside the shade of a row of palm trees. Unsure of what I wished to find, I turned and kept on walking. Then I saw it, the first sign of people.

A hundred meters from where I stood was a smattering of rural homes. Unsure of whether I should go to them, I assessed my options and found my choices shrinking. I had to take the chance and so I did. Without jogging, so as not to cause alarm, I walked briskly toward them, and as I did, I quickly saw a group of people. Just outside the third home were women, five or six, sitting in a kind of circle. They wore the traditional hijabs with their faces showing, and they all stared back at me.

"Marhaba [hello]," I said as I drew nearer. "I am a little . . . if you could, where is the highway?"

"Where do you want to go?" an older lady asked.

"The highway," I said.

"My boy, you can't get to it from here," she said. "You have to turn around and then go straight."

I was crestfallen. The last thing I wanted to do was turn back in the direction I had come from.

"How?" I asked.

"Go there," she pointed back to the bend in the lane, "and take a right and carry on straight. A little while, and you will see it."

"Thank you," I said, and as I strode away, I could hear them whispering behind me. *Just get there*, I thought. Past the corner, out of sight, and I started running.

For the following ten minutes, I would walk, jog, and run, covering as much distance as I could without stopping or toppling over. And just as my energy was all but sapped, I saw it. Past a solitary house, up the sloping ground, a half mile or so away from me. *Surely that is it.* My heart pounded, and I found myself close to weeping. *Keep going.* With tired legs, I pedaled on, swerving drunkenly as I bounded forward. My mind so awash with the cries of desperate wanting that I failed to hear the door of the solitary home open, noticing only after a man had walked some yards toward me.

I glanced in his direction and slowed my steps, but kept on moving. "You," he shouted, drawing in closer. I carried on. "Who are you?" he asked, and I slowed and looked at him. In his mid-fifties, he wore a white dishdasha and black dusty shoes. Unless I chose to ignore him or run, there was no way to avoid talking to him, so I stopped.

"Where are you going?" he asked when he got to me.

I pointed a hand to the road. "Is that the highway?"

"Where are you going?" he asked again as he stood close in front, his eyes studying me with the utmost curiosity.

I was breathing deeply, and I tried my best to control it, to not arouse suspicion. "I want to get to the highway," I said.

He nodded for a second, thinking, before his tone changed a little, "Where did you come from?"

"I did not come from . . ." I began to say, "I just want to get to the highway."

While we were speaking, two other men stepped out of the house. They were younger, somewhere in their twenties, and before I knew it, they had come to us, and all three stood in front of me. "You," one of them asked, "from where did you come?"

My mouth opened to speak, but I stopped it, unsure of what words to choose. And all the while, I could feel their eyes tracing over me. "I was here," I finally said. "They let me go, and . . . I am going."

"Who took you?" the father quickly asked, and there seemed little point in lying.

"I don't know. Believe me, I don't know. I just want to get to the highway."

"Look," he said, "you go that way, and they will kill you."

"Who will kill me?" I asked.

"My boy, no one comes out here at this time, you understand? Anybody they see on the highway they will kill."

"Then let them kill me," I said, and as I did my eyes suddenly noticed it, a small mobile phone in his hand. "If you would give me your phone," I implored, "then I will call someone, and they will come to get me."

He stood there considering the proposition, as one of the sons leaned in to whisper something to the other. There are moments in life when you need something, some stroke of luck to fall your way. Every fiber in your body wills it, a seed balancing on a knife's edge, and where it drops makes all the difference. That was one such moment, and I was about to have another.

"Who are you going to call?" he asked.

"My brother," I quickly answered.

"Take it." He stretched out his hand, and I grabbed the phone. There was only one problem.

As a result of the bombing two years previously, all the landlines in Baghdad had been destroyed. It was a fact known by all, and thus for two years, no one ever attempted to use them. Instead, people opted for mobile phones, which were still operational. My problem was that the only mobile phone number I knew from memory was my own. The very same phone that I was carrying on the day I was taken.

Standing there, I held the phone while my mind raced about frantically for a number to dial. But there was none. A few seconds ticked by, and I felt him staring at me inquisitively, wondering what it was I was doing. Slowly I began to punch the keys, and thus came that other moment.

The only number I remembered was the landline, which by all odds would not be working. The one at the home that was previously my father's, where my eldest brother's family lived. The phone beeped as I keyed in each digit, prayed for a miracle, and pressed the speaker to my ear.

Please God.

Static.

Nothing.

Maybe they have fixed it. Perhaps it takes a second to connect. And then.

"Hello." Agavni, my brother's wife.

"Agavni," I said without pausing, "this is Saad. Where is Ardwan?"

"ARDWAN," she began to scream, over and over again, and in between her shouts she kept asking, "Where are you?"

"Get Ardwan." I said. "Get him now!"

I heard the breath-like rub of the handle, the shuffle of movement.

Please God.

"Saad?"

"Yes, come for me on the highway."

"Which highway?" he asked.

"Just come to the Dora. Like you are coming to the seminary."

"But where?"

"Don't worry, just drive that way, and I will be waiting. I will find you."

Before my brother could answer or ask another question, I closed the phone and placed it quickly in the hand of the man in front of me. "Thank you, uncle," I said, and without a second's hesitation, I hopped a few steps before I took off running.

"Where are you going?" the old man shouted. "They will kill you." But there would be no more stopping. The highway was out in front, and all I had to do was cross it.

The ground sloped up, and I pumped my legs. There was no more room for pain; my mind was far too busy. I glanced to the side, checking for cars, and when I saw there were none, I jumped onto the road, scurried across it, and dove down the other side. This was where I had to be. I could not be fully sure, but if I knew roughly where I was, then at some point my brother would have to pass me. The rest of the time would like many others be spent waiting.

In those days, a curfew was in place in Iraq. It did not come into effect until midnight, and the hour was closer to nine in the evening. Yet the traffic usually began to decrease a while before it had to. That, coupled with the notorious nature of the area in which I had found myself, meant that there would be few cars passing. Still, I remained as vigilant as I could be. I ran for five more minutes before stopping. There, aided by the darkness and the sloping ground, I lay quite hidden, ten meters back from the highway.

My brother's car was a blue Opel Vectra '98 with narrow lights and a long front body. He had had it for some years, and I felt confident I would be able to spot it. Surely, he would have left quickly, I thought, as I attempted to calculate how long it would be before he reached me. Another twenty minutes or so, I reasoned.

Three cars came and went as time spun on, and I remained half hidden. Peering to make sure none was my brother's, and ducking back again.

Soon. My God soon.

Then a sound from afar like a wave washing up on shore. A car was coming. It could be him. I crawled up to the side of the road, squinting at the brightness of the lights as they hurtled toward me.

Closer, and still I could not tell.

It seemed like it could be his car, and I searched frantically for a way to be sure, but as it passed, I quickly saw that it was an old Mercedes, and I ducked back down to wait.

A few minutes more, and another passed along. I could see it was too large. Then I saw one, far in the distance. It was going fast but not quite as fast as the others, and that strange unexplainable feeling began to itch inside me. Onward it came. Closer. And I still could see nothing either to confirm or rule it out. Once again I stood, staring far and stepping forward as the car continued, unveiling more of itself the closer it got to me. Breathlessly I waited. The moment drawing closer. Down to mere seconds, and just like that it passed me, and I thought I saw him.

Running on the road, I screamed and jumped, my arms waving high above me. "Ardwan. Ardwan," when suddenly the car stopped and began to turn around.

It had to be my brother. The car came close. I glanced inside and there he was. Reaching for the backdoor, I yanked it open and dove inside. "Go!" I said. "Just drive. Go!" And the car sped off again.

Ardwan was driving, and a friend was sitting beside him, gun in hand. "How are you?" he kept asking, but I was out of words just then. There was none left in me. "Not now," I said, my voice small and shuddering, "just take me home."

There is little more from that drive that I remember. It would have spanned forty or so minutes, but I was done counting. The rest of that night was made up of Polaroids of scenes that I was both in and absent from. My brother and his friend were speaking, but all I heard was sound as I lay my head on the backseat cushions, struggling to convince myself that it was truly over.

When we finally arrived at home, my brother parked the car and rushed to help me out. My legs could barely stand any longer. It was as though my whole body had been held up by thin sticks of scaffolding that had all suddenly collapsed.

The front door of the house was already open. Slowly we walked, and I was still holding myself up. For all that time until then, by the teeth of will, I had kept myself together. It was not until the moment when I limped inside and my mother held me in her arms that I finally surrendered. I wanted to tell her that I was alright but I couldn't. Just as I had dreamed in those darkened hours, I wanted to tell her that she need not worry any longer, but we simply stood there weeping. Tears of joy and sadness.

Upon hearing the news, some of our neighbors had gathered in my mother's living room to greet me, but I was in no state to see them. "What do you want?" my brother asked.

"I need to bathe," I said, and as the people left to go back to their homes, my brother gently walked me to the bathroom. We stepped inside, and he closed the door behind us.

I could see him watching, his face clenched with the resolve of being strong for me, of helping, of doing the things that needed doing. It was only when he removed my clothes, when he saw the lines and lines of peeled flesh and bruising, all along my legs and back and shoulders, that he could hold it in no more. I slid slowly down into the hot soothing water as my eldest brother broke down crying beside me.

CHAPTER 15

The Answer

On some early evenings, I would hop in the car with my sister and we would drive to St. Raphael Hospital in central Baghdad. My father's nursing shift would be close to ending, and he would make his way to meet us by the door. We would drive through Abu Nawas street, passing by the people who crowded outside its many restaurants and cafes, played dominos, and smoked shishas until the morning hours. And then we too would stop for a brief while. The three of us, drinking fresh cold juice and speaking of everything and nothing in particular.

Time was bending once again. As I lay in that very same hospital on the day after my release, I found myself inside those memories, and they flickered in the distance, a lifetime ago and yet very close beside me.

I did not stay there long. Everything was fast that first week, after it had ended. The sisters who ran the hospital tended to me kindly. They fussed and fretted over me, they drew blood and ran the tests they needed. Nothing permanent. No irreparable damage that time would not heal. No broken bones, just cuts and heavy bruises.

The following morning, I was back at my mother's home. I had shed in excess of twenty kilos of body weight, and my energy was slow in returning. Even the lightest of exertions came laden with troubles as my joints ached incessantly. My back and knees were the worst, and it would be months before I would begin to think of them as fully mended. The rest took longer: too long to pinpoint to a given day.

Two weeks later, on the sixth of October 2006, exactly three years after I had first returned to Iraq, I left again for Italy. The patriarch suggested that I take some time, collect myself, and give thought to perhaps continuing my studies. That was what I decided to do. The road to my doctorate degree was longer and more winding than I could ever have imagined, but eventually I got there.

Even when I was out of Iraq and its turmoil, I had not truly left where I had been or what I had gone through there. Sudden innoxious sounds would filter through my senses like the bang of a bullet. The door slamming or the creaking of windows when the wind was blowing. All such sounds would make me jump and cause the muscles in my neck to tense. After all the days of danger, it was not easy to convince myself that I was safe.

Ten years have now passed, and such thoughts have long faded. The specifics of those days rarely find me any longer. I do, however, think of those I met, not so much the ones who lied and tortured me, but those few who unveiled a glint of kindness inside the black of cruelty. Who could have done little or less, but chose the more in spite of all the dangers. I fear and hope for them, and I always will. The rest of the memories come when some trigger causes the trapdoors of time to open: a news item that dredges up something familiar, threats and explosions, stories of abduction and ransom. Even when I am watching a movie, some scene will jump out at me and take me there. Perhaps I will see a helpless, handcuffed man huddled in some dirty corner, and, for a brief time, I will return to the one I occupied.

Beyond that, I do not dwell on the details, but instead view it all as one episode of time that I can stand back from and look at. Staring not as the man who was first hustled into the car on that Tuesday afternoon but as the one who emerged a month or so later. That is the thing with such experiences. The you that they become a part of is transformed by their presence. It is as though the pen with which you write the story of your life suddenly runs dry, and no word that comes after will ever be of that exact color.

I often asked to know the purpose of that journey, what God's intention could have been in placing me where I had found myself. Why, when I had come with no other reason than to help, would I have been ushered off to die in some field or river.

The design of God is far larger than me or any one of us. God did not compel those men to take me, just as he did not compel the countless others who have chosen to be the catalysts for tragedy. Ours is the burden of decision. That is the price of our freedom. The reason for an experience is not like a stationary box, wherein lies its meaning, but is an invisible force as malleable as thought. Often we cannot help but feel a certain way about a particular thing, and the reason for it comes from our choice of action.

For me, I have again been reborn into my purpose: to tell others that faith need not wilt in the face of difficulties but can blossom, offering greater clarity, that a belief in the love of God compels us to see the love in one another; to not separate those who believe from those who do not; to not judge one faith to be above another but to see that some people can find a rationale for violence from religion, while others find a rationale for unity.

In 2009, after earning my doctorate in philosophy, I returned to Baghdad. The situation there was much as it remains today, stuck in a whirlpool of corruption and violence. Though l cannot but hope for a better tomorrow, I am utterly saddened when I consider how realistic such an expectation is. The country's descent continues as the numbers of the dead climb ever higher. How many years and how many lives must be paid for a lasting peace and for the end of bloodshed? I shudder to wonder, and ask myself how we have ever let it come to this. I know that we are all somehow at fault, that we played a part in what happened.

We live in times of untold danger: where the month I spent in captivity is but a drop in the ocean of sorrows endured by countless others; where brothers and sisters, fathers and mothers, sons and daughters are continuously killed and victimized in an expanding cycle of barbarism.

A lady once stood up to ask me how, in the current climate of this world, one can realistically preach that people should turn the other cheek.

Love. I used the word often, and yet it is one of the few for which there is no substitute. At its essence Christianity is love, and love is not surrender. It is not to meekly endure, nor is it to blindly turn away from those in grave need of assistance. When his holiness Pope Francis endorsed the use of military force to halt the systematic persecution of Christians and other religious minorities in Iraq, he did so with warning. That force be used to stop the unjust oppressor, that it not be used as an excuse for a war of conquest.

These are delicate times with no simple easy solutions. Love must be the driving force for all people, to "love your enemy," to look beyond the threats of the here and now, to look beyond ethnicity, creed, culture, or religion, and to connect on a level of shared humanity.

It is the mission of love that Christ has asked of us, and every day and every hour it rises up to challenge us. It is the mission for which I have dedicated my life, along with so many others. It is the mission I will carry with me for all time, whether I was a Priest or a Bishop, whether I lived in Iraq or elsewhere.

We see it now in the world around us, in the many forces that oppress the notion, in the voices that dismiss it as fanciful and unrealistic, in the never ending onslaught of wickedness and cruelty. We see fear and hatred close at hand and are tempted to paint love as weakness.

Christ is love and love was never meant to be easy. It is the hardest thing of all and yet it will always be the only answer.

Appello del Papa per il rilascio di un sacerdote rapito in Iraq

Un accorato appello per la liberazione di un sacerdote cattolico di rito caldeo sequestrato, martedì 15, a Baghdad, è stato lanciato da Benedetto XVI in un telegramma — a firma del Cardinale Angelo Sodano, Segretario di Stato — inviato a S.B. Emmanuel III Delly, Patriarca di Babilonia dei Caldei. Ecco il testo del telegramma:

Deeply saddened by news of the abduction of Father Saad Syrop Hanna, the Holy Father wishes me to assure Your Beatitude and all the pastors and faithful of the beloved Chaldean Church of his spiritual closeness and prayerful solidarity. His Holiness makes a heartfelt appeal to the abductors to release the young priest at once, so that he can return to the service of God, the Christian community and his countrymen. The Holy Father's thoughts also go to all the victims of abduction in your Country and he prays that this dreadful scourge, as well as the "terrible daily bloodshed which delays the dawn of reconciliation and rebuilding" (*Angelus* of 15 August 2006) will finally come to an end. His Holiness encourages the members of the Catholic community to continue to work together with all religious believers and people of good will towards a future of harmonious and respectful coexistence for the beloved Nation of Iraq.

Cardinal ANGELO SODANO
Secretary of State

SAAD SIROP HANNA

is the Apostolic Visitor for Chaldeans Residing in Europe,
the auxiliary bishop of the Chaldean Patriarchate of
Baghdad, Iraq, and visiting researcher in the Medieval
Institute, University of Notre Dame.